Dedication

To our students, the faculty and our friends at Chapman University who provide such a great forum for new thoughts and new ideas.

To our families, who tolerate us as we grapple with new thoughts and new ideas.

For our very patient families and for our students, faculty and friends at Chapman University.

Table of Contents

—⟨⟩⟨⟩⟨⟩—

Preface

———∞———

*There is always a well-known solution to every human problem
– neat, plausible, and wrong.*
—H.L. Mencken

The current income tax system in the United States of America is under siege. It should be. It is too complicated for too many Americans and insufficiently robust to insure collection of an appropriate amount of taxation from the most successful in our society. Reform is necessary. In fact, it is crucial. The current tax system penalizes productivity and burdens honest Americans with an enormous cost of compliance as well as a certain dread whenever the Internal Revenue Service comes calling.

How difficult is the current system to understand? The Secretary of the Treasury ran into a hurdle when he was nominated by President Obama for his job because he had failed to understand the tax code's treatment of his earnings while working for the International Monetary Fund. That's right, the senior member of the President's cabinet charged with supervision of the national economy couldn't figure out the tax code's application to his own earnings.

But—there's always a but—we are both concerned that any reform that comes be <u>good</u> reform, not terrible reform, and that the political momentum behind tax simplification not be wasted on pie-in-the-sky schemes that wouldn't work even if they could be enacted.

Economists and political scientists both recognize the truth of Gresham's Law, which holds that the presence of bad money in the economy will drive out the good money. Thus coins that are supposed to be pure gold that are in fact adulterated with some non-gold substitute will drive the pure gold coins out of circulation. No one wants to get paid with diluted coins or pay with the real coins when the counterfeits are moving through the system. The good money goes into hiding.

Just as bad money drives out good money, so will bad tax reform drive out good and necessary tax reform. It stands to reason that there's only so much oxygen in any room when the talk turns to tax reform, only so many people are interested in it, only so many legislators willing to work for it and journalists willing to cover it.

Today, a very well financed organization is promoting a woefully simplistic and economically dangerous tax proposal that they call the FairTax. The hubris of calling their own tax proposal the "FairTax" should not be lost on the reader. Despite the nom de plume selected, the FairTax is anything but fair. Indeed, it is so thoroughly flawed as to make the Internal Revenue Code appear to have been provided to us by a higher authority. This book is about the FairTax and the nightmare that it would present to the American public if enacted. Public officials who know this have to stop hesitating when the subject comes up for fear of being thought anti-reform. The FairTax is a reform killer, and needs to be exposed as reform fraud. Politicians who endorse it for the easy energy it brings them from grassroots who are hazy on the details, but who hate the IRS and the current system need to learn to speak clearly in favor of reform, but against the FairTax fantasy. Republicans especially have to discipline themselves to both advance serious tax simplification and reform while refusing to pander to noisy activists enamored of a scheme that can't work, won't be adopted, but which will lead the GOP down a garden path ending in defeat and disillusion.

As you will see in the pages that follow, the claims of the FairTax proponents are often just silly, and when confronted thereon, the initial response, more often than not, is to attack the critic as stupid or biased rather than confront the issues raised. This has made an honest, robust and constructive discussion regarding the FairTax virtually impossible to conduct. This book is an attempt to put both information and accuracy into the public domain.

The authors believe that successful tax reform must significantly reduce the complexity of the Internal Revenue Code for 90 percent of the public while retaining a significant and necessary level of complexity for the ten percent of individuals and businesses doing complex transactions. This is the only manner in which our government can successfully collect sufficient taxes to operate our nation and have a reasonable level of compliance from the bulk of its citizens. Successful tax reform must not litter the country with additional bureaucracy, or provide new and ripe opportunities for increased tax fraud or initiate trade wars throughout the world. Successful federal tax reform cannot drive already hugely expensive state and local government budgets into the stratosphere. The FairTax would affect all of these bad results and more besides.

The authors are not economists. Adler is an accountant, who after a long and very successful career in public accounting with Deloitte & Touche is now a professor in the George Argyros School of Business & Economics at Chapman University. Hewitt is a professor of law across the street at Chapman's law school, where he has taught Constitutional Law for a decade and a half while also conducting a career as a broadcast journalist on television and radio. Both have read widely in the literature about the FairTax. Many of the commentators on the FairTax, both pro and con, are accomplished economists and consider the technical issues with respect to the FairTax in terms of price levels, accommodations by the Federal Reserve , and mathematical permutations and models which even the highly informed public cast aside as irrelevant to the debate. Of course these specialized critiques are not irrelevant to the wisdom of adopting the FairTax, but they are indeed of secondary importance. The proponents of the FairTax are offering primarily political and equity arguments in defense of their sweeping proposals, and we are responding on that level. If the reader desires an analysis of the economic models that predict the economic future of the United States with appropriate pricing models after a FairTax, this book is an introduction, but the specialized literature is available.

This book is also not about the size and scope of the federal government and what the authors view as runaway federal spending and continuing encroachment of the federal bureaucracy into far too many aspects of our lives. We recognize the importance of these issues and leave that discussion for another day and other books. Hewitt's credentials as a Reagan Republican cannot be seriously debated, and he vouches that Adler is just as traditionally conservative as any policy wonk likely to be found wandering the halls of the Heritage Foundation or the American Enterprise Institute. We agree with a lot of the assumptions of the proponents of the FairTax, so we aren't going to cover that ground and weigh down this book with needless rhetoric about all that's wrong with the country.

This is a book about what is wrong with the FairTax. No more and no less. If the media and politicians would do their jobs, it wouldn't be necessary. But they haven't and the FairTax fantasy has spread.

Finally, we want to end our preface with a note on tone. Hewitt last saw Neil Boortz, one of the great voices of talk radio and a primary architect of the FairTax movement, at the White House on January 13, 2009, when they and some of their broadcast colleagues spent 75 minutes discussing with George W. Bush the past eight years of his presidency and the challenges ahead for incoming President Barack Obama. Hewitt and Boortz were both there because they see eye to eye on so much, and share an esteem for much of the work that George W. Bush had done over the very difficult years of his presidency. Hewitt told Boortz, as they waited in the Roosevelt Room to enter the Oval Office, that this book was imminent and that he was looking forward to the debate. Boortz was ready to get it underway then and there, and in a tone that suggested it would be a rollicking conversation between respectful adversaries.

And so we hope it will be. Neither we nor the FairTax advocates are in the business of pulling punches, and we expect this will go 15 rounds. There are a lot of FairTax fans out there, and we aim to convert many of them to the cause of genuine tax reform. We hope as well to pry Mike Huckabee and others away from the campaign crack cocaine that is the adulation of the FairTax shock troops.

But, at the end of the day, we need tax reform so that the enormous energies of the American economy can be unleashed in all their vigor and put to the end of building a second American century.

Hank Adler

Hugh Hewitt

Chapter 1

Three Bob's

—⊗⊗⊗—

If I were a rich man,
Ya ha deedle deedle, bubba bubba deedle deedle dum.
All day long I'd biddy biddy bum.
If I were a wealthy man.
I wouldn't have to work hard.
Ya ha deedle deedle, bubba bubba deedle deedle dum.
If I were a biddy biddy rich,
Yidle-diddle-didle-didle man.

—From Fiddler on the Roof

"If I were already a rich man and earning a bloody fortune as an actor, athlete, Wall Street titan or whatever" Hank told Hugh as they first began to discuss this FairTax in 2008, "the most important thing in my life would be to help pass the FairTax."

The fairness of any tax system is generally measured by how it impacts certain groups of people. The country is full of different economic segments and business sectors, and hundreds of "levels of income," and we cannot possibly examine the impact of the Fair Tax on them all, so we need to look first at its impact on some representative hypotheticals. For this effort we have selected three "Bobs" to illustrate the uneven nature of the impacts of the FairTax on different economic elements of our society.

The first Bob, let's call him "First Bob," is among the super rich. You can decide whether First Bob is a Wall Street titan, a rock star, a professional athlete or an individual that inherited a significant fortune. Whatever Bob did (or did not do) to create his wealth, today he owns a home in New York, and three vacation homes—one in Hawaii, one in Sun Valley, Utah, and a third outside of Paris. He also owns a small fleet of vehicles, a yacht and has investment assets with a value of many hundreds of millions of dollars. Including his business income and compensation for whatever profession you chose, First Bob has an annual income of $10,000,000.

First Bob has what many believe to be "the good life," but the tax code bothers him. It pursues him. Believe it or not, he cannot escape it, though many myths suggest he lives a life surrounded by accountants and lawyers that keep Uncle Sam from his vault, First Bob is indeed surrounded by accountants and lawyers, but they can only do so much. Hank has represented more than few of these folks over the years, and try as he might, the law gets its share of First Bob's income.

Under the current federal income tax system, First Bob pays about $3,200,000 in federal income taxes. He and the other super rich in the United States, the top one percent of taxpayers, pay about one-third of all U.S. income taxes. You may not want to believe that, but it is true.

Under the proposed FairTax rate, First Bob would have to buy over $13,900,000 of new goods and services for consumption ***within the United States*** to pay $3,200,000 of federal taxes, the amount of federal income taxes he is currently paying.

Trust us, First Bob supports the FairTax. Actually, First Bob <u>really</u> supports the FairTax, talks about it to his friends, buys copies of the books extolling the Fair Tax and sends them to the candidates he contributes to, and often rocks himself to sleep at night thinking about the possibility of a FairTax and his federal tax burden effectively going away. He views the FairTax as a personal plan with which he can create inter-generational wealth rivaling the feudal era.

First Bob knows that under the FairTax, if he can keep his consumption in the United States limited to $400,000 a year, a pretty serious figure, he can keep his U.S. taxes to about $90,000 a year. He can then invest the remainder of his funds tax free, and he would purchase any big ticket item that would require a FairTax in the United States in a country where there is no FairTax. Generally, he would keep these items outside the United States although he would "slip" the small ones into the country. The Rolex vendors in the U.S. are out of business the moment the Fair Tax passes, as are the dealers of small planes, yachts, craftsman furnishings and designer dresses. All gone. The very, very wealthy did not get or stay that way by paying unnecessary taxes.

First Bob would also know—remember those lawyers and accountants— that after the passage of a FairTax, if he buys yet another home that had been built before the date of enactment of the FairTax, he would pay no FairTax on the purchase. First Bob would know that if he buys yet another new or used vacation home in Switzerland or a new chateau in France, he would pay no FairTax. He knows that if he buys agricultural land for investment in the United States, he would pay no FairTax. He knows that if he buys a new home for investment, he would pay no FairTax and if he buys that new home for an investment, he would pay 30 percent less for that new home than a new homeowner. (Trust us, that's how the Fair Tax is supposed to work—no Fair Tax on new properties purchased to rent as investments, but the full Fair Tax on homes purchased to live in.)

First Bob knows that paying his maid and/or gardener subjects him to a FairTax and that he is responsible for filing FairTax forms and self employment forms for them. Of course, if First Bob is at all shady and pays his maid and gardener in cash, they can split the savings by not paying the FairTax. Like most of our readers, we condemn tax cheats like First Bob who pay their help off-book, but we know they are legion and we know they aren't going away after the enactment of the FairTax with the IRS gone.

Paying the help under the table is a win for First Bob because he saves money, and a win for them as First Bob can pay them more. The maid and gardener, if they are legal residents, will continue to receive their monthly payments from the government (the FairTax calls these checks "Prebates") even though First Bob is paying them under the table.

Under the FairTax, First Bob's taxes could easily be reduced by $3,110,000 per year plus, when he passes away, his entire estate would pass to his children tax-free with the elimination of the estate tax. Hugh supports the elimination of the Death Tax, but most Americans, among them Hank, want it retained on estates over $10 million. First Bob certainly wants it abolished. Under the FairTax it is gone and First Bob's family would avoid an estate tax of well over $200 million. First Bob also receives a monthly tax-free payment from the United States government (his Prebate) to offset any FairTaxes he must pay until he spends an amount equal to the U.S. poverty rate. Winner, Winner, Winner!

Second Bob is a resident of another country. Second Bob is either an international athlete, an international entertainer, or an international banker. Let's actually pick Second Bob's profession and make him the reigning heavyweight champion of the world. Second Bob is a resident of Monaco, a country without an income tax. Bob is going to fight for the heavyweight championship of the world in Madison Square Garden. Bob's pre-fight plan is very simple; he would fly to New York on Monday morning, book a few rooms in a prestigious hotel, and fight the challenger on Saturday evening in front of a full house and an enormous world-wide audience on pay-tv. On the following Monday, with $100,000,000 in his pocket, he would return to Monaco. Under the current Internal Revenue Code, Second Bob would leave behind about $32,000,000 in federal income taxes. Under the FairTax, Second Bob might incur a few thousand dollars of U.S. taxes. Second Bob also thinks the FairTax is a pretty good idea.

Let's call third Bob "Regular Retired Bob." Regular Retired Bob earns $17,000 from his savings. Regular Retired Bob and his wife annually receive $30,000 from Social Security. They own their home. Regular Retired Bob and Mrs. Bob contribute $1000 per year to their church. Under current law, Regular Retired Bob & Mrs. Bob pay no federal income taxes and are subjected to no payroll taxes. Regular Retired Bob and Mrs. Bob annually spend all of their income plus $10,000 of their savings and therefore spend about $56,000 per year on goods and services for consumption in the United States. Under the current federal income tax system, Regular Retired Bob and Mrs. Bob have $56,000 in purchasing power.

Under the FairTax, Regular Retired Bob and Mrs. Bob would receive $4402 annually (their "Prebate") from the federal government to offset the FairTax's imposition on the goods and services every

American needs to live at or below the poverty level. (This is in addition to their Social Security benefits.) They would thus have $60,402 to spend on goods and services for consumption under the FairTax, but their purchasing power would be ***reduced significantly***. They would only be able to purchase only $46,509 of goods and services while paying $13,892 in FairTaxes. Their purchasing power would be reduced by $9,491 or about 17 percent under the FairTax. This is because they would move from a literally no federal tax regimen under existing law to a federal FairTax on every purchase of goods or services they make. One can safely say that Regular Retired Bob and Mrs. Bob are not going to be big fans of the FairTax.

There are 300,000,000 different Bob's in the United States and the impacts on every category of individual are different under the FairTax. Hank Bob and Hugh Bob think the FairTax would be pretty good for each of them, but that's not what matters. What matters is the impact of the FairTax on the entire country because Hank and Hugh—like most of you—genuinely enjoy living in the U.S. and count themselves blessed to have won the world lottery when they were born here. We worry about radical plans that, despite the best of intentions, overturn larger parts of the laws of the country and in so doing destroy the assumptions that have seen people build it up, and wreck the engine on which that prosperity has long depended.

Suffice to say that any new tax system is going to create winners and losers. We have concluded, after long and careful study of the FairTax as it is proposed by its leading apostles, that there will be many more Regular Retired Bobs than First or Second Bobs and that that is important because the Regular Retired Bobs and the millions of Regular Working Bobs are going to be paying the federal taxes which the First and Second Bobs would no longer have to pay.

We also think it is unconstitutional.

We hope this brief illustration puts you on notice that a whole lot of folks ought to get very angry when the FairTax people start extolling their plans because those plans will punish them for having played by long-established rules. There are millions and millions of losers under the FairTax, and we think the country as a whole is a loser as well. To understand the FairTax, one needs not only to study the "Bobs", but to also understand the impacts of the FairTax on the entire economic system. With this understanding, one can look through the various claims and counter-claims about the FairTax and make an educated decision about whether the FairTax is good or bad for the United States of America.

Chapter 2

A Summary of the FairTax

—❄❄❄—

The FairTax proposal that we critique in this book is the one popularized by radio talk show host Neal Boortz and Congressman John Linder in a 2005 book titled, simply, *The FairTax Book*. The FairTax Act was introduced in Congress in 2005, 2007 and 2009 by Congressman Linder and has many co-sponsors. Former Arkansas Governor Mike Huckabee endorses the FairTax and campaigned on it in Iowa in 2007 and 2008 and beyond in the presidential primaries of 2008. A second book was published by Boortz and Linder with Rob Woodall in February of 2008, *FairTax: The Truth: Answering the Critics.*

Our criticisms of the FairTax are based on the plan as it has been proposed by Boortz and Linder. The quick summary of the FairTax is that it is a plan that creates a national sales tax on all goods and services at the retail level. It would replace all federal individual and corporate taxes, Social Security and Medicare taxes and the estate and gift tax.

The legislation establishing the FairTax would also establish a "Prebate", a monthly payment from the federal Treasury to all U.S. citizens and legal residents to offset the federal sales taxes (the FairTax) paid for goods and services purchased with income below the poverty level, as determined annually by the federal government. This is a feature designed to avoid the charge and reality of taxing the poor who already struggle to survive without a massive new sales tax on nearly everything they purchase. (We believe the FairTax legislation has an "oops" in their calculation of this amount.)

After reimbursing—in advance—citizens and legal residents for the estimated sales taxes levied upon the dollar value of estimated necessary retail expenditures at the estimated national poverty level, all lawful citizens would pay a flat rate national sales tax on all purchases of retail goods and services.

The proponents of the FairTax have created great controversy and confusion by describing their FairTax as a ***23 percent tax***, calculated on a **"tax-inclusive basis"**. This description has created great controversy and confusion because generally sales taxes in the U.S. are described on a **"tax-exclusive basis."** If you and a friend are talking about the sales tax you pay in your state, you are talking about the "tax-exclusive" sales tax. This difference in definition of terms has huge consequences for the conversation that follows, so let us quickly illustrate it for you now.

If your state has a 9 percent sales tax, and you buy a $100 table at Ikea, you will pay $109. That's "tax-exclusive" talk.

If you speak "tax inclusive" talk and your state is collecting a $9.00 tax on that same $100 table, you will pay the same $109 total price and that $9 tax will be referred to as 8.2 percent tax.

A 23 percent FairTax calculated on a "tax-inclusive basis" is equal to a 30 percent FairTax on a "tax-exclusive basis". An item on which the seller receives $100 costs the buyer $130 under the FairTax. The tax is the same $30 whether calculated under either a "tax-inclusive" or "tax-exclusive" basis.

We think it is fraudulent to call the FairTax a 23 percent tax when the vast majority of Americans who hear 23 percent think 23 percent in tax-exclusive terms. We will use tax -exclusive calculations throughout this book because we seek to clarify, not confuse the issue. Voters should ask themselves why proponents of the FairTax adopt a strange approach to language and thus sacrifice clarity at the outset of the debate.

The proposed rate of tax has also created great controversy. Studies prepared by the proponents of the FairTax have concluded that a 23 percent tax on all goods and services at the retail level calculated on a "tax-inclusive basis" (equal to a 30 percent tax calculated on a "tax-exclusive basis") would be almost equal to all the taxes currently collected from the taxes to be eliminated: the individual and corporate income taxes, payroll taxes and the estate and gift taxes. But other, very persuasive studies have shown that a "tax-exclusive" rate approaching 50 percent would be necessary to replace all the lost tax revenue. It still might make sense to replace the current system with a sales tax of 50 percent, but the public would recoil from such a dramatic shift in pricing. Again, we prefer clarity. We believe the studies that are not put forward by FairTax proponents are the ones to trust, and there is ample independent analysis from credible economists not affiliated with the FairTax organization. We believe that a sales tax approaching 50 percent on the goods and services to be taxed under the FairTax proposal would be what is necessary to replace lost revenue.

The proposal to provide the monthly "Prebate" to only citizens and legal residents has also created great controversy in some constituencies. Obviously the large illegal alien population of the U.S.—somewhere between 12 and 25 million, depending on whom you trust when it comes to demographics—will be devastated by a sudden sharp increase of prices. They and their families and supporters will brand the FairTax for what it is, a huge burden-shifting to the poorest of the poor. Critics of illegal immigrants will cheer at the prospect of devastating the economic incentives to come to this country and will argue that the FairTax will force millions to return to their countries by impoverishing them even more than they are already.

The thought of subjecting this population, which to some great extent already lives at or below the poverty line, to at least a 30 percent increase in prices overnight would create a large handful of moral, financial and law enforcement issues. On the moral side, is the United States of America going to institute a "let them eat cake" policy with respect to the Prebate? On the financial side—is the federal government going to be forced to provide the Prebate to illegal immigrants via court ruling? On the law enforcement side, is there going to be greater crime if illegal residents suddenly find their earnings are reduced by 30 percent and they find they move from barely feeding their families to not feeding their families? Are there going to be increased non-payment of rents as food prices explode? The idea of rolling the dice with this sort of approach is among the most irresponsible public policy proposals of all time, right up there with demands for an "open border" between the U.S. and Mexico, the sort of proposal that flows from zealotry, not careful rational weighing of options to improve the country's future.

There are more huge problems. Exports, for example, would be exempted from the national sales tax. The proposal to exclude exports from the FairTax launches a thousand ships, each one loaded with problems.

Nations which import U.S. goods that are suddenly free of that part of their pricing previously made up of U.S. taxes would see the devastation of their domestic industries that produce goods that compete with the U.S. exports. Suddenly the Japanese television maker is faced with an avalanche of cheap U.S. televisions, and the pricing advantage for U.S. exports envisioned by FairTax proponents would apply to the millions of products the U.S. exports from every type of screw to every make of automobile.

FairTax proponents haven't thought through the reaction of the world to such a bald attempt to rewrite the rules to favor U.S. exports. Our trading partners would respond with very legitimate complaints to the World Trade Organization **_and_** with increased tariffs on imported goods from the United States. Welcome to the trade war to end all trade wars.

The international trade implications of the FairTax are very complicated and pose macroeconomic questions not discussed in this book. But we know they are there, and we know the rest of the world isn't going to applaud and then welcome a unilateral trade advantage for the U.S. FairTax proponents seem to believe that the U.S. can simply force the rest of the world to go along, perhaps shrugging their collective shoulders and adopting their own version of the FairTax. We are realists. This is the trade equivalent of Russian Roulette. Too many American jobs and families depend on export growth to simply say "It will work out in the end."

There are some pretty practical issues as well on this side of the border. Residents of other countries would be able to purchase goods from the United States at prices significantly lower than those available in the U.S. A tractor exported to Mexico and purchased there for $40,000 would run $52,000 in San Antonio, Texas. The farmers of the

United States might not think this is such a great idea, especially if they grow crops that compete with Mexican crops.

Then there is the huge problem of the FairTax's treatment of investment property. Property purchased for investment would be exempted from the 30 percent sales tax. New housing purchased for the purpose of living in it is, however, subject to the FairTax. This distinction causes more than a few enormous consequences.

The investment buyer—be that buyer an oligarch from the Soviet Union or First Bob—would not pay the FairTax. The new homeowner would be required to pay the FairTax. Hence, a new home where the builder has set a price of $300,000 would cost the investor $300,000 and that same new home would cost the resident-buyer $390,000. Think about how such an enormous disparity would impact the housing market, creating a huge incentive for developers to build homes for landlords, not for homebuyers.

Under the FairTax, states would face very significant cost increases because the FairTax requires state and municipal governments to pay the FairTax on state salaries and purchases. Each year the 50 states and their local governments make hundreds of billions of dollars in government purchases and payment of salaries, which the day after the FairTax is enacted will require a 30 percent larger budget. There are only two ways for a state to raise that money—by begging it from the feds (who are cramming this tax upon the states) or by levying new taxes on their home state populations. The FairTax would also eliminate the non-taxable borrowing opportunity for state and local government, exposing these entities to additional annual interest costs of even more billions, a giant wreck of state and local government and finance systems. "Don't worry," the FairTax sirens sing, "It will all work out." (We believe this aspect of the FairTax scheme is unconstitutional by the way, but leave that subject for another place.)

The FairTax would be administered by a local "State Sales Tax Administrating Authority" in each state which would, along with collecting the tax and registering every lawful state resident, provide resident data to the Social Security Administration to enable the Social Security Administration to mail the monthly Prebate checks to each legal resident in the United States. If a state or states choose not to administer the FairTax, the federal Department of the Treasury would become the "Sales Tax Administrating Authority" in such states. The Treasury Department—wherein resides the current Internal Revenue Service— would have general rule making responsibilities. Meet the new boss, as the song goes, same as the old boss.

This is just a quick overview of the major provisions of the FairTax, a sort of starter course in FairTax fantasy, intended to break the spell of the inviting, indeed enticing simplicity that the FairTax myth makers have built up. In our age of complex financial institutions and ridiculously dense regulations, the lure of the hammer and the smash-up is huge, but also deeply destructive. Look around the country. For all the problems with the recession of 2008-9, the current tax code and especially with the high levels of taxation, the country is an economic giant and by far the strongest nation not just on the globe but ever in recorded human history. Maintaining that dominance is a key goal for every generation that wants to leave their children even greater opportunities. The reckless indulgence of half-baked pieties is a recipe for disaster, and the FairTax is just such a recipe, though "half-baked" is too kind a description.

Chapter 3

The FairTax Rate is 30 Percent

—∞∞∞—

A Rose By Any Other Name. . .
—Shakespeare

We have made this point before, but we will make it again and again: Contrary to the continuing distortion by the proponents of the FairTax, the tax rate proposed under the FairTax plan is 30 percent. Again, despite the rhetoric of the FairTax lobby, the FairTax proposes a federal national sales tax rate of 30 percent.

The proponents of the FairTax intend for the federal government to collect an amount of federal revenues under the FairTax in an amount equal to current federal collections of federal income taxes on both corporations and individuals, all social security taxes and all estate and gift taxes.

While this chapter explains that the FairTax proponents proposed 23 percent FairTax rate is in reality 30 percent ("reality" defined as the use of terms and descriptions that convey the tax as virtually anyone on his planet thinks about sales taxes), there is also great debate as to what FairTax rate is required to collect taxes equal to the taxes to be eliminated. Federal government research and some highly qualified independent researchers believe the FairTax rate may need to approach a rate as high as ***50 percent*** to make up for the federal taxes proposed for elimination. (Note that this rate is exclusive of existing and as discussed later, almost certain additional state and local sales taxes)

So, given that ordinary taxpayers would quickly conclude that the FairTax levies a 30 percent sales tax, why do the FairTax proponents tell us that the tax rate is only 23 percent? You guessed it: It is much easier to sell a 23 percent sales tax than a 30 percent sales tax.

To get to the 23 percent number, the FairTax rate is calculated by FairTax proponents on a "tax-inclusive" basis. Not one of 45 states that have sales taxes describes their sales tax in "tax-inclusionary" terms.

If you know the difference between a "tax-inclusive rate" or a "tax-exclusive rate", you are either an academic or deserve a spot in the final round of Jeopardy. It is unlikely that your CPA, if you have one, could define the terms off the top of his head. No one, absolutely no one, who wanted an audience of average Americans to understand the cost of the FairTax would describe the tax using this "tax-inclusive rate." But clarity is not a goal of the FairTax proponents.

Let's put an example on the table: Assume that you are standing on the bridge of a ship in Boston Harbor and selling me a crate of tea. Assume that you are going to sell that crate of tea to me and after the government gets its taxes, you want to receive $100.00. How much am I going to need to pay you for the crate of tea under the FairTax for you to get your $100?

Under the FairTax, I am going to pay you $130.00 and the government is going to take $30 in taxes. (There is no debate on the amount of the tax; it is $30. FairTax proponents will agree on the amount of tax that would be assessed.) But they say that $30 of $130 is 23 percent of $130. The vast majority of Americans would say, however, that a 30 percent sales tax had been assessed on the tea as the seller sets $100 and the government gets $30.

Put another way, a" tax-inclusive" rate means that the tax is measured against the ultimate total price paid including the sales tax. 23 percent of $130.00 is $30. For you as the seller of the tea to determine the proper price so that you receive your $100, you would need to divide the amount of funds you are going to keep by .77. Not many merchants are going to welcome this pretzel logic and pretzel tax calculation, but the FairTax band wants you to play by their music.

Everywhere, be it New York City, Los Angeles, Anchorage or any city in East Africa, all sales taxes are calculated, reported and understood on a "tax-exclusive rate" basis. When we talk about sales tax, we think cost first, then we find out what the sales tax rate is and multiply the cost times the sales tax rate to get to the sales tax. In our example above, the cost is $100, the sales tax is $30 and we consider it a 30 percent sales tax rate.

Again, if you live in a state where there is a sales tax, it is calculated on a "tax-exclusive" method. (This is not "most states", this is <u>all</u> states with a sales tax.) Let's put the same example on the table with a 10 percent sales tax as understood in every state that collects sales taxes.

Assume that you are back standing on the bridge of that same ship in Boston Harbor and selling me a crate of tea. Assume that you are going to sell that crate of tea to me and you are going to receive $100.00. With a 10 percent sales tax, how much am I going to pay you for the crate of tea under your state's sales tax method?

That's right. I am going to pay you $110.00. You calculated the tax rate to be 10 percent in a nano-second because this is how we think and talk about sales taxes. Well, that's how everyone thinks and talks about sales taxes <u>except</u> the FairTax folks. If the FairTax proponents described your sales tax under their "tax exclusionary rate", they would tell you that the $10 sales tax is a tax rate of 9.09 percent. They would be academically correct and you would likely look at them like they were nut cases.

Why do the FairTax proponents tell us that the tax rate is only 23 percent? That is, as we said above, a very interesting question.

We believe that describing the tax rate on a "tax-inclusive basis" is both misleading and inappropriate. Intentionally or unintentionally, the "tax-inclusive" calculation has led millions of Americans to think the FairTax rate is less than it would actually be in practice.

The FairTax advocates argue that the FairTax is calculated in the same manner in which the federal income tax is calculated. That is, that the federal tax is paid from your taxable earnings and is therefore calculated on a "tax inclusionary basis". This is technically correct, but completely beside the point. We want people to understand how the new tax system would work if the FairTax was adopted. We want clarity so the public understands the trade-offs being proposed. Everyone already knows how much they pay in taxes under the current system—or at least they can find out with some careful calculation. Even if they miss some crafty taxes—like those assessed on airplane tickets etc—they know generally what the tax bite is that they are paying. And they generally know how the system works.

Most of us think of our federal tax as not based on our gross income, but based upon our taxable income. Most taxpayers orchestrate their personal situations to insure that their taxable income is as low as possible. This is built into our culture. It is a learned behavior, deeply embedded in our decision making. We know, for example, mortgage interest is deductible and figure that into what sort of house we can afford to buy. We know that contributions to charity are tax deductible and the size of our donations is impacted by that knowledge.

If we adopt a FairTax, we will have to rewire our decision making, and we would. But in considering whether we want to go about that rewiring, we have to be very careful to keep the public informed of the new rules, and especially the new rates. Because our current tax-paying culture calculates sales taxes in the "tax-exclusionary" method, honest debate will use that method.

The fascinating question as we mentioned several times above is why when virtually anyone who spends a bit of time trying to understand the FairTax and concludes that the tax rate is really 30 percent, why the FairTax people insist that the calculation must be made *their way?*

We know the proponents of the FairTax will object that our standing firm on this issue and that our insisting on the discussion at 30 percent is simply a tactic to try to make them look bad. It is rather a tactic that prefers clarity which has the effect of exposing not just the real sales tax rate proposed, but also the important revelation that FairTax proponents begin the debate with an attempt to obscure and confuse.

Neal Boortz, in ***FairTax: The Truth*** responds to the critics of this purposeful confusion this way:

> *"So how do these opponents and skeptics come up with the 30 percent figure? By playing on the confusion that exists between an inclusive and an exclusive sales tax. That's how. This confusion is exacerbated by the fact that virtually every one of the forty-five*

states that collect a sales tax computes that sales tax on an exclusive basis. That's the difference: the FairTax is computed on an inclusive basis. It's as simple as that."

So, all forty-five states that have a sales tax compute the their sales tax on a tax-exclusive basis, but the opponents of the FairTax who wish to use the same method are the problem. Read Neal's defense again. It is wonderful. It is bold beyond description. It is also, of course, side-splittingly absurd.

There is one last note to make on this debate, a key one that explains why FairTax folks are so adamant on this issue, even to the point of obvious absurdity.

A hard truth about the FairTax fantasy is that the FairTax rate proposed by the FairTax proponents is significantly <u>less</u> than most independent calculations of the necessary tax rate to raise the same dollar amount as raised under the current federal tax system. If you are persuaded by those studies, you will want to get a new number to use to describe the tax rate at which the FairTax will have to be set to achieve tax revenue neutrality.

Here's the kicker. The gap between "tax-inclusive" and "tax-exclusive" grows larger as the tax rate rises. The difference at the proposed rate is 7 percent—23 percent and 30 percent.

But if the 23/30 rate isn't enough to collect the same amount of revenue as currently collected, the disparity between the two rates gets larger (and thus more stunning if you use the tax-exclusionary methodology.) If FairTax proponents ever get around to admitting that they need a higher rate to achieve revenue neutrality, they will most definitely want to use their own rules. Say they conceded a "tax-inclusionary" methodology required a 37.5 percent sales tax rate. In the real world—the world we live in—the sales tax would be 60 percent! Get it? They want a methodology that protects them from sticker shock if their defense on revenue neutrality crumbles.

So much for what the FairTax rate is or is not. The FairTax rate is 30 percent, as proposed by the sponsors. And that rate won't raise the revenue the government already spends.

Chapter 4

The FairTax:
Truths About Its Consequences

———— ∞∞∞ ————

S o, if the FairTax fantasy ever came to pass, what would the impacts be on your life? On your parents' lives? On your businesses or the businesses of the people who employ you? Part of the powerful lure of the FairTax fantasy is the apparent simplicity of its approach, but the consequences of its passage would be anything but simple.

Prices must surely increase with the FairTax and the price increases would be significant. Most of the FairTax folk will admit this though some, including Governor Huckabee in interviews with Hugh, refuse to concede this obvious point. In a Tax Notes article dated November 13, 2006 (p. 677) by serious pro- FairTax economists entitled: Taxing *Sales Under the FairTax, What Rate Works?*, they admitted the obvious, that "consumer prices would rise by roughly 30 percent."

If you are paying federal taxes–income taxes, payroll taxes, gas taxes—you will, of course, pocket the sum you are presently sending to the federal government, and that will cushion the blow of a dramatic price hike.

But if you are retired, there is no new offsetting source of income to afford or subsidize the new tax. This is simply a reduction in purchasing power. One of the reasons the FairTax is a political fantasy is that the very organized, very powerful senior citizen lobby will never allow it to get close to reality given the undeniable consequence of reduced standards of living among the already-retired if the FairTax enters into operation.

If you are working, the elimination of income tax withholding and social security from your payroll check should partially offset the increase in prices. For the wealthy who are employed, the elimination of these taxes will more than offset the tax increase resulting from the FairTax. For those who have withholding of over 30 percent of their salary, there would be a net increase in monthly purchasing power; for those with salaries where withholding is under 25 percent, which appears to be most Americans, there will be a reduction in purchasing power. This would be somewhat offset by the Prebate.

The elimination of the federal income tax would have wide-ranging effects on every taxpayer and taxpayer group in the United States. The impacts would neither be universally positive for any group, save for the super rich, nor universally negative for any group, though the middle class will almost all lose money under the scheme.

For those seniors or near-seniors that have worked hard and saved during their lifetimes, there are some very interesting and disturbing results. At implementation, existing savings accrued with an eye on projected retirement costs will instantly lose an enormous amount of their purchasing power. Seniors who had planned on a low tax lifestyle via the rigors of planning and investing –and after paying taxes on their income for entire lives and saving for retirement—would suddenly be facing a huge new federal tax, taking the place of the income tax they had long labored under. Talk about bait-and-switch. This would be the most dramatic instance of double taxation in our history. Imagine all of one's savings for retirement being effectively reduced in value by almost 30 percent, in a single day, as the result of a new "FairTax" on all purchases. Then try and imagine elected officials facing down the AARP-mobilized armies of senior citizens.

Now forget the image of millions of seniors dialing their Congressmen and consider other aspects of the impact of the FairTax scheme. What's the proposal do to purchasing power generally?

The chart below shows the impacts upon savings from the FairTax at two separate tax rates. The percentage decrease in value remains the same as the money is already in the bank of the retiree.

	Federal	Federal
	Tax-Rate	Tax-Rate
	15%	34%
Pre-FairTax Earnings	$1,000	$1,000
Federal Taxes Paid Years Earlier	150	340
Cash At Implementation of FairTax	850	660
FairTax on Purchases	255	198
Purchasing Power	$595	$462
Reduction in Purchasing Power After FairTax	$255	$198
Percentage Reduction in Purchasing Power	30.00%	30.00%

What is truly frightening about these numbers is that the purchasing power of existing savings nationwide would be reduced by at least 30 percent and there is no virtually discussion about the issue by the proponents of the FairTax. Bruce Bartlett, an economic policy advisor to the first President Bush raised this issue and received a chilling and candid response from Laurence Kotlikoff an economist and proponent of the FairTax in a paper entitled "Why the Fair Tax Will Work" dated January 15, 2008: "*Well, rich members of today's older generations may be a concern of Bartlett. They aren't a concern of mine.*"

Kudos to Mr. Kotlikoff for candor, but the world of politics is a world that takes very seriously "rich members of today's older generation," as well as the millions of other Americans who have been saving for years whether or not they are "rich" or older. The attempt to minimize the huge impact to accumulated savings by suggesting it is only the concern of the old and the rich is not only unpersuasive, but it also part of a pattern of dismissiveness and defensiveness that marks the rhetoric of some FairTax proponents.

With respect to future earnings or income under the FairTax, calculating the impact on an individual's purchasing power is difficult because every federal income tax return is different and average rates of tax can be difficult to calculate. To determine relative purchasing power of future income and receipts one needs to determine the gross income of the individual and actual purchases at retail. But we know for sure that high income earners will want the FairTax adopted as soon as possible.

As we noted in our introductory chapter, at the highest income levels, current federal income taxes approximate 32 percent (after deductions for state income taxes). If a hypothetical athlete/actor/software inventor earns $50,000,000 from salary and endorsements, his or her approximate federal income taxes would approximate $16,000,000.

It would be virtually impossible for a highly paid athlete or actor to spend sufficient funds under a FairTax system to equal their current federal income taxes. To pay the same amount of taxes with a FairTax, our professional athlete or actor would need to make FairTax retail purchases in the United States of goods and services for consumption of over $69,000,000, and that simply isn't going to happen. As a result, the high wage earner is going to have a dramatic reduction in federal taxes and will have funds to invest far in addition than under the current Internal Revenue Code. There is no more classic example of the rich getting richer than the absurdity of subjecting them to a consumption tax.

Proponents of the FairTax argue that the vast tax savings among the very wealthy will produce significant increased investment by the previously heavily taxed wealthy, and therefore new jobs and a much more dynamic economy will follow. Increased economic investment may occur, but one undeniable reality is that someone other than the wealthy will be paying these lost taxes while the wealthy make their investments. This is confirmed by the promise that FairTax revenues will equal revenues under the current law.

While the proponents of the FairTax promote the plan's fairness by noting the inability of the wealthy to plan around the FairTax, the ultra-rich certainly would be able to do so, and pretty much so will everyone else who can find a friend abroad to do some shopping for them. The very wealthy will simply go abroad to make their high end purchases. Think of the opportunity to purchase goods outside the United States. The cost of a new vacation home in the United States increases by 30 percent under the FairTax while the cost of a vacation home in Europe, the Caribbean, or Canada would be paid for with untaxed U.S. dollars a vacation home would be an easy decision. The foreign vacation sailboat which could have previously been built by U.S. workers in Seattle or Maine would now be subject to the FairTax while the sailboat built elsewhere would be purchased with untaxed U.S. dollars. Goodbye U.S. builders; hello foreign craftsmen.

The FairTax proponents anticipate spending very little on auditing of Americans etc., and they propose that Americans will simply declare all out-of-country purchased goods. Right! The answer to any high dollar purchase under the FairTax for the tax cheat currently cheating on his federal income taxes would be to purchase items overseas and then transport them back to the United States or to have someone else make the purchase overseas and sneak it back into the United States. Want a Rolex? Have a European friend purchase it and wear it across the border, where you will meet him and reimburse him for his trouble. Today, the US. Government cannot stop illegal immigrants from crossing into the United States by the thousands every week. Why would we think that we could stop untaxed goods from crossing the border is a very difficult question. Tax cheats at the high end aren't going to suddenly become law compliers because the federal income tax went away.

Let's turn next to the American dream –buying your own home.

The key FairTax concept to grab onto is that an investor who buys a house for the purpose of renting it will not pay the FairTax on that purchase. The buyer who intends to live in the home will pay 30 percent on the purchase price.

The FairTax places the investor at an incredibly significant economic advantage relative to the taxpayer who wants nothing more than to buy a new home and live there. A home where the home builder will receive $300,000 is going to cost the buyer-resident $390,000 as $90,000 will be paid to the federal government as a FairTax. That same home would cost an investor $300,000 because the investor's purchase is untaxed under the FairTax. (This, of course, assumes the FairTax rate of 30 percent and that the individual states are not forced to abandon their existing sales tax regimens and adopt the FairTax for their own state. No state currently taxes new home purchases, but as discussed elsewhere, the FairTax puts the state in a position that would probably force the state to adopt its own FairTax.)

If we assume for the moment that the FairTax rate is 30 percent and the new sales tax in the state is an additional tax-exclusive 15 percent, the cost of that house for the new homeowner would be $448,500. ($300,000 x 1.15 = $345,000; $345,000 x 1.30 = $448,500). It would still be $300,000 for the investor.

The FairTax provides that an investor purchaser of a new residence would not be subject to the FairTax. The result is that the investor buyer would have a 30 percent price advantage in competing with the home buyer for new residential property under a FairTax without an accompanying state FairTax and an almost 50 percent advantage if there is an accompanying state sales tax of 15 percent.

The investor-purchaser is going to have a huge amount of leverage in bargaining with the seller of the new home, including the ability to pay a premium and will pay significantly less than the resident-buyer.

The huge advantaging of the investor-owner over the owner-occupier would have far reaching consequences for our society. And given the fact that rents would be subject to the FairTax, we also note it would create a huge incentive to fraud between investor-owners and their tenants. How many investors would suggest to renters a discount for rent paid in cash? The FairTax fraud department just got larger again.

The list of unknown effects has just begun. All of the social and business incentives, benefits and disincentives included in the Internal Revenue Code disappear under the FairTax. These include the following with the social benefit shown and in some cases an example of a problem that could occur immediately or in the future:

- *Mortgage interest and property tax deductions, which encourage home ownership, vanish.*

Millions of homeowners are paying little or no federal income taxes as the result of their home interest and property tax deductions. For these taxpayers, while a FairTax represents an elimination of Social Security and Medicare taxes only, an accompanying 30 percent FairTax on all purchases could put them into bankruptcy. The homeowners' mortgage interest will not disappear on the day the FairTax appears, just the deduction and the accompanying reduction or elimination of his federal income taxes he or she counted on when making his purchase.

- *Individual retirement plans, self employed pension plans, pension plans for businesses encourage saving for retirement by providing a tax advantage for contributions made to them.*

The Internal Revenue Code encourages individuals to put money aside for retirement. This is a classic case of the tax code promoting good public policy. The FairTax leaves Social Security in place, yet provides no additional incentives to save for retirement. We doubt very much that retirement savings will approach anything like its current level when the tax advantages disappear.

- *The Charitable deductions encourage contributions to charity*

While there is some evidence that <u>most</u> taxpayers do not determine to make their weekly church contributions etc. based upon the deductibility of their contributions, there is significant evidence that the <u>wealthy</u> are influenced greatly by the Internal Revenue Code with respect to significant gifting. There is also significant evidence that the charitable activities of the wealthy are the key to the health of many of our most important institutions – colleges, medical facilities, the arts. To the extent a wealthy individual gives $20,000,000 to a local non-profit university or hospital and receives a tax deduction with a value of $7,000,000, that represents $13,000,000 of spending that the government needs not fund. Most, if not all, wealthy charitable contributors look to see the "after-tax" effects of their giving and make their decisions accordingly. The not-for-profit sector will fight tooth and nail the moment that the FairTax seems to be approaching reality, and with good reason. One of their huge fund-raising advantages will disappear overnight, and their missions would be severely compromised. Again, part of our argument is that political realities will prevent a FairTax advancing and that proponents of genuine, achievable tax reform should not waste energy and money on the FairTax fantasy. Contemplating a campaign against the combined memberships of the country's most popular charities and medical institutions, not to mention many churches, should drive home the political impossibility of the FairTax plan.

- *Adoption credits in the tax code encourage adoption.*

The social benefits of encouraging adoption ought to be self-evident.

- *Lower tax rates on capital gains and dividends encourage investment & savings.*
- *Energy credits encourage the protection of the environment through the conservation of energy.*
- *The deduction for casualty losses lowers taxes after calamity*

The American tradition of helping Americans out during unanticipated catastrophe disappears under the FairTax. All reductions in taxation after unforeseen events disappear: Whether it be a mass Ponzi scheme such as Bernard Madoff's, a fire in a mobile home park such as in Los Angeles, or a hurricane such as Katrina in New Orleans, the United States has an historic tradition and an underlying income tax code that softens many of the worst financial blows through a reduction or elimination of federal taxes. None of this is possible under the FairTax. The individual who has lost everything, under the FairTax, would still be faced with the same 30 percent FairTax on every purchase for houses and other items destroyed.

- *The deduction for medical expenses lowers taxes during serious illness*

The issue that causes the largest number of personal bankruptcies in the United States is catastrophic illness. Despite the widespread availability of health insurance and charitable care, catastrophic illness and the high cost of medical care is a major problem for U.S. taxpayers. One safeguard against the potentially staggering cost of medical care has been the deductibility of costs over 7.5 percent of income in the calculation of taxable income. The FairTax not only eliminates those deductions, the FairTax puts a tax on medical services.

- *Deductions & credits are provided for child care costs under the current tax code, making it possible for many lower income parents to earn a living and feed their families*
- *Foreign tax credits ensure that Americans working abroad are not double taxed on their income.*

If an American goes to work in Europe and pays income taxes in Europe and returns to the United States, he is not double taxed on his income as the Internal Revenue Code provides for a reduction of his federal tax based on the foreign taxes he has already paid. Under the FairTax, he will pay his foreign taxes overseas, send his after-tax earnings to his family in the United States and they will then be subjected to the FairTax. This effective tax rate would be confiscatory.

- *At implementation, high earning citizens with deferred income from such items as stock options would have immediate increases in purchasing power as they would receive the funds without paying any federal taxes.*

Think about an entrepreneur with literally millions of untaxed stock options who would currently pay a 32 percent income tax under the current law upon exercise (purchase and immediate sale) of the company's stock. Under the FairTax, the exercise of these options becomes tax free and a 32 percent benefit of possibly tens of millions of dollars falls to the entrepreneur. Many with significant stock options will be an ally of the FairTax plan.

Any individual who has had the economic ability to defer his income for federal income tax purposes in tax advantaged deferred income investments would recognize what anyone would refer to as a windfall profit upon the passage of a FairTax.

The authors know a now sixty-eight year old lawyer who has put as much as possible into his Individual Investment Retirement Account for decades. His annual "contributions" to his IRA have completely and properly avoided all federal taxation. With successful investments which have gone untaxed, he has invested wisely and accumulated a large sum in this account which has never been taxed. He has always believed that all of this money would eventually become available to him tax-free because someone would make the income from the Individual Retirement Accounts tax-free. His belief has been that those with the gold always win and under the FairTax, he gets both confirmation of his thinking and the gold.

- *At implementation, investors would have the ability to sell investment assets without federal taxes. The proceeds of such gains would be immediately available for reinvestment without any federal tax consequence. Thus those with sizeable investments will cheer the FairTax.*
- *Many very wealthy individuals that have invested in real estate for their entire lives have never paid federal income taxes on the appreciation of their assets. For these individuals, the only tax to which they would currently be subject is the inevitable estate tax. The FairTax eliminates the estate and gift tax thereby allowing these individuals and their heirs to have avoided income taxes during both their entire lives and at the point of death.*
- *At implementation, citizens would be able to make unlimited gifts to their children without tax consequences and estates of any size would be able to be passed from one generation to the next without federal taxation.*

This is an interesting issue. Currently, the income tax and the estate and gift taxes implicitly make it difficult for great wealth to be passed generation to generation. Not impossible, simply difficult, because the lawyers and accountants and financial planners are somewhat effective in helping wealthy taxpayers avoid at least portions of the estate tax (although often, this is through charitable contributions, with the funds going to charity rather than to heirs).

The current federal estate and gift tax law taxes only the wealthiest of our society (though the new Obama Administration and Democratic Congress seem poised to again apply the estate tax to relatively small estates.) Virtually everyone else is exempted from the current estate and gift taxes. This would not be the case under a FairTax. Once an individual family managed to earn more than it was spending, the investments would pass tax free generation to generation, creating a permanent "upper class" in the United States far wealthier than that which exists today, and the gap between most Americans and the economic aristocracy would grow much more rapidly and much larger under the FairTax.

- *Existing alimony decrees and agreements would become a serious problem as such decrees and agreements contemplate increased buying power for the payor of alimony through tax deductions and decreased purchasing power for the recipient through the receipt of alimony being taxable income.*
- *Claims to the contrary, for many individuals, the compliance requirements of the FairTax would be significantly increased.*

Service providers, investors owning property, and people performing part time jobs would be required to file monthly sales tax reports with the new state or federal authorities charged with collecting the FairTax. Proponents of the FairTax argue that overall the compliance burden will drop dramatically, but even if they are correct in their best estimates, many individuals will find themselves stuck with compliance issues they have never before borne.

The list of consequences is endless because the FairTax proposes a revolution in the way government revenues are collected, incomes accumulated, and the prices of everything determined. Just a few more examples should convey just how great a leap in the dark is being urged on us by the FairTax folk:

- *The FairTax will tax items which have historically been sales tax taboo. Buyers will face federal sales taxes on food, electricity, trash collection and medical costs. When these taxes are applied to items for which the buyer has no remedy except to purchase, the reality of the FairTax will be very, very far from the hype.*
- *Some industries will be severely impacted by the FairTax. Consider any business that serves the tourist from abroad The cost of visiting the United States increases by the FairTax rate. Sure, many will still come to see the Grand Canyon, or sample San Francisco's*

wonders. But not as many, and those that come will be spending far less when they do. The tourism business would be in for a huge shock if the Fair Tax was adopted.

The Fair Tax and its economic impact on different economic groups will not be neutral. Clearly, wealthy individuals will be huge winners. Within all other economic groups, the results of the Fair Tax will vary dramatically depending on many choices made during a lifetime such as "rent or own", leverage or not, spend or save, pension or cash compensation. Each reader will need sort through their own situation.

The proponents of the Fair Tax hate to admit that the complexity of the modern economy has birthed a necessarily complex tax code, but ignoring this doesn't alter the reality, and the politicians that advance the cause of the Fair Tax should be willing to sit and answer the thousands of questions that their radical approach raises.

Chapter 5

The "Prebate" –
An Explanation/Analysis

———— ∞ ————

*Every Legal Resident Receives A Monthly Check –
Warren Buffet and An Unemployed Auto Worker Receive
the Same Amount*

The FairTax scheme provides that all lawful residents receive a monthly check from the federal government, a "Prebate." The Prebate is supposed to be equal to the sales taxes imposed on the expected retail purchases of an individual or family at the poverty level, and is thus a way of keeping the very poor from being injured by the imposition of the national sales tax that the Fair tax envisions. To assure that there is no fraud, everyone gets the Prebate, though it increases as the family size increases. The amount of the Prebate will not be impacted by the income or wealth of the recipient. Everyone gets it, and if you ask why Bill Gates needs the Prebate, the answer is that he doesn't, but that the "simplicity" of the system does.

Because of the Prebate, proponents of the FairTax believe that the FairTax is not a "regressive tax," meaning one which burdens the poorer members of the country more than the richer citizens. That's absurd nonsense, because the FairTax acts regressively the moment the first dollar is spent above the total amount of spending above the poverty line. At that point, the tax is 100 percent regressive. This is not an opinion, it is a fact.

The idea of "regressive taxes" is difficult for some people to grasp. Simply put, a dollar is more valuable to a poor person than a rich person. The poorer you are, the more you need money because life requires certain purchases. The technicians will explain that a tax is regressive if the portion of income paid in taxes decreases as income increases. The authors would tell you a tax is regressive if the tax impacts the buying decision of the poor and does not hardly impact the buying decision of the rich.

The FairTax provides that this Prebate would be paid monthly to all lawful residents with a Social Security number regardless of income, age, wealth or any other constraint. (No payment of any amount is provided for unlawful residents—illegal aliens.) This lack of means testing is bizarre, but part of the selling of the FairTax has been to push radical simplicity in its administration. No income test for the Prebate enhances that simplicity.

Under our current tax system, we have none of the incredibly burdensome administrative complexities of the Prebate system. As you will see, the FairTax which is flawed is so many other ways, brings along a level of administrative complexity to successively pay the Prebate in the right amounts to the right people on a monthly basis that it makes administrating the current federal income tax look as simple as bringing in the morning newspaper. Perhaps surprisingly, the cost to government of administrating the current income tax would be significantly less than administrating the FairTax.

"Lawful residents" include all legal temporary residents that qualify for a Social Security card. Legal residents could include individuals working at the United Nations, individuals in the United States for college and anyone else that has established legal residence in the United States and has a Social Security number. Wealthy citizens as well as wealthy temporary residents and the poorest of the poor of our society, if legal residents, would receive exactly the same Prebate.

The Prebate sounds wonderful, and who doesn't like the idea of getting a check from the government each month? But the practical problems are enormous, even if you can get past the idea of hitting the "just above the poverty level" folk with a massive price hike on all the goods and services they purchase.

First, all purchases of retail goods and services would be taxed at the FairTax poverty-level rate of 30 percent, but the Prebate is expected to cover only the increased cost of the purchase of necessities. There is, however, no mechanism to ensure that the Prebate would be spent for the necessities of the individual or his family. There would be no assurance that a child would not go hungry while the Prebate funds are spent on drugs, alcohol or chocolate bars. This is the primary reason that the federal government food stamp program exists—to assure the taxpayers that the cost of the public assistance is actually used for food. Imagine the mom struggling to feed, clothe and obtain medical care for her children if the husband has any sort of dependency problem which soaks up the check coming from the government straight to him. Her costs just shot up, but the money she needs to pay for that increase takes a permanent detour through her husband's bank account.

Then there's the problem of inflation and price surprises. The "poverty level" is an annual calculation by the Department of Health and Human Services. It is not adjusted during the year and makes no adjustment for events that take place during the fiscal year. In times of general inflation, or when specific goods skyrocket in price, the Prebate would stay fixed but the cost of the goods and services would rise, as would the tax imposed on them. We had a taste of this in the summer of 2008 when gas soared to over $4 a gallon. If the FairTax had been in effect that summer, gas would have cost $5.20 a gallon, far more than the $2.60 it cost in January of 2008. And of course, while the price of gas was increasing, the FairTax would have been hitting every penny of price increase. During this period, however, the Prebate would <u>not</u> have adjusted. The budgets of those near or below the poverty level, already devastated by the soaring cost of gas , would have been shattered to an even greater degree under the Fair Tax, and the Prebate would have stayed fixed until 2009.

Then there is the enormous problem of the impact of the FairTax on illegal immigrants. This isn't a book about what to do or not do about the 12 to 25 million illegal immigrants in the United States. But it is clear that the FairTax would devastate the finances of people in the country illegally. That may be fine with you, but it will shock the conscience of many, and make passage of the FairTax as drafted impossible. The illegal immigrant with children –legal or not—will get nothing, but will see the price of food go up by 30 percent or more. It is doubtful that illegal aliens would even seek the Prebate for their legal children, bringing them, as it would, to the attention of the government they are trying to avoid.

The FairTax plan provides that the Prebate is to be paid to qualified families living in a common residence: All family members sharing a common residence shall be considered as part of one qualified family. The monthly check goes to the head of the family.

The FairTax will replace income tax planning with qualified family residence planning. Moving a family member into a separate residence will increase the total Prebate for the family. If grandpa lives in the same home as his children, the annual Prebate from having him in his children's home would be $749.80 in 2005 dollars, but if he lives on his own in his own residence, it would be $2201.10. So, how could schemers get the extra Prebate money? They could swap grandpas, (at least on paper). If, on paper, our grandpa lives in apartment A and we live in apartment B with whom the schemers traded grandpas, our family picks up additional Prebate payments of about $1500. The same is true for the family in apartment B. The government will never figure out who lives where; we will just swap grandpas on paper so they have separate addresses and if the government comes to check, we will move them into the other apartment for an hour. Obviously, we are not condoning fraud, but the probability of such behavior is so high it needs the spotlight. The Prebate rules are hopelessly simple, meaning easy to manipulate.

The cost and scope of the Prebate administration are covered later, when the administration of the whole scheme is considered. But quickly note that that the auditing and registration issues under the Prebate are huge. The family unit issues alone would present administrative issues that we believe cannot be solved. Anyone with any knowledge of the welfare system's complicated rules concerning families knows, that there is no magic wand to wave that will suddenly take the complexities out of the enormously complicated and varied ways in which Americans manage to live in family units.

The first step in the Prebate process envisioned by the FairTax folk is the registration of all legal residents. It is no secret that there are zillions of phony Social Security cards in circulation. How the agencies would deal with these issues is problematical. Whether the Social Security Administration, despite the legislative requirement in the FairTax statute, would have the resources or the interest to do more than random samples is an interesting question.

The FairTax would also immediately further <u>decrease</u> incentives for states to cooperate with immigration authorities. Every fraudulent registration and therefore fraudulent prebate check would increase federal tax dollars flowing into a state. Auditing a family to determine whether the family was entitled to receive their Prebate would be economically counter-productive for the state under any circumstances. The cost of the audit would exceed any potential revenues. We believe that there would likely be significant fraud at the Prebate recipient level because successful fraud would create an income stream that would especially tempt the hard-pressed, and there is not any part of the system with a stake in exposing that fraud.

We also note that the notion of paying a Prebate to any non-citizen is certain to be controversial, raising the prospect of either more obstacles to passage or eliminating the inclusion, but the latter change would add more complexity to the system.

One of the glaring oversights of the FairTax is that despite claims to the contrary, the FairTax does <u>not</u> provide the poor with a payment equal to 100 percent of the sales taxes they would pay at the poverty level. The reason for this appears to be that the drafters of the legislation got mixed up in their own foot work with respect to their tax-inclusive rate nonsense.

In The FairTax Book, a chapter is entitled "The FairTax Prebate: The Key to Fairness" In that chapter, Mr. Boortz writes:

> The folks that wrote the FairTax plan knew the burdening the poor with a 23 percent retail sales tax would doom the plan from the outset. And since the FairTax was designed from scratch – as opposed to the hodgepodge of rules and regulations we call the income tax – its creators ensured that no one should ever have to pay the sales tax on the basic necessities of

life. That's why the prebate – the monthly check covering taxes on all basic household necessities – was invented.

Well, as the legislation is actually drafted, everyone will pay a significant portion of the sales tax on the basic necessities of life. As we said, that is because the drafters of the language got caught up in their own "tax-inclusive" versus "tax-exclusive" nonsense. The drafters doomed the poor with a 23 percent <u>tax-inclusive FairTax</u> and a 23 percent <u>tax-exclusive Prebate</u>. The result is that the Prebate comes up $714 short of covering the FairTax on the basic necessities of life for people at the poverty line.

The calculation that is provided at the FairTax.org website at the time of our writing provides that in 2008, a poverty level single person could be expected to purchase $10,400 of goods and services and would receive a "Prebate" of $2392 . What this means is that at the poverty level, a single individual would be expected to purchase, pre-Prebate, various goods and services worth $10,400. After the law enters into effect, he would receive his Prebate check of $2,392 to offset the 30 percent hike in prices because of the Fair Tax. But the cost of those goods would be $13,506 and the total of income and Prebate is only $12,792.

The calculation that is provided in The FairTax.org website at the time of our writing provides that in 2008, a poverty level single person could be expected to purchase $10,400 of goods and services and that person would receive a "Prebate" of $2392. What this means is that at the poverty level, a single individual would be expected to purchase pre-Prebate various goods and services worth $10,400 without exceeding his Prebate amount. These purchases would produce a total "tax-inclusionary" price by the seller of $13,506 and a FairTax of $3106. The poverty level buyer would therefore be short by $714.00 in being able to purchase his poverty level of goods and services.

So, let's be clear, the prebate does not pay 100 percent of the sales taxes for goods and services purchased by those at the poverty level. It only covers 77 percent of those taxes. Oops. This is the kind of error that gets into utopian schemes because no one takes them seriously.

There has also been little or no discussion about Prebate payments to the homeless, and no wonder. It is a very difficult segment of the population to care for or even keep track of. Getting them their Prebates is another logistical nightmare, but their cost of staying alive will go up 30 percent nonetheless. It is hard to imagine that any group that deals with the care and recovery of such individuals and families won't be vocal opponents of the FairTax. They join the ever growing mass of not-yet-mobilized opponents of the scheme who would come out of the woodwork to punish the party that seeks to move the fantasy to reality.

We close this discussion of the Prebate by reminding you that the FairTax plan envisions the states as the key operators of the system. Each state that opts in as the administering agency would have to develop software to register every legal resident and their family status annually. Think about your most recent engagement with your state's Department of Motor Vehicles. Perhaps it went well. There are many superb employees in the various state DMVs, and often the systems work well and flawlessly. But very often they don't, and long lines and headaches have marked many a visit to the DMV.

Well the number of employees and the cost and complexity of the software required to be a FairTax administering state dwarf those of the DMVs. Ask yourself how well you think that is going to work out.

Chapter 6

Exports

———— ⚬⚬⚬ ————

If I live in Mexico, the Chevy produced in Michigan
will cost me $20,000. If I live in Michigan,
that same Chevy costs $26,000

The FairTax isn't charged on exports.

The simple optics of not charging a FairTax on exports are difficult to accept.

Can anyone think it is a good idea for a head of California lettuce to cost less in London, including shipping, than in Salinas, California where it is grown?

When Hank's children were fairly young and something would go woefully wrong, as things often do with young children, he would ask them: "Ok, don't tell me what you were thinking, tell me *if* you were thinking." The idea of politicians arguing for voters to elect them so that they can enact a system under which Mexicans and Canadians will pay 30 percent less than Americans for everything America makes or grows and sends to those countries is wildly amusing. Suicide politics, of course, but amusing.

The consequences of export exclusion are pretty difficult to forecast, but here is one example of a plausible scenario of price action under the FairTax.

We assume, as argued earlier and also conceded by some FairTax proponents, that post-enactment prices will rise 30 percent or more.

Currently a computer costing $100 in the states costs $102 in England because it costs $2.00 to ship the product overseas. Assume the cost of production is $80. The after-tax profit on the sale of both computers is $20. It doesn't matter to the producer where it sells the computer.

If, under the FairTax, we sell our product in the United States, to achieve our $20 after-tax profit, we now need to sell the product in the United States for $129.87. If we export the product to Europe, to achieve our after-tax profit, we continue to need to sell the product in Europe for $102.00. Let's review these numbers:

	Current Pricing & Profit	
	U.S. Sales	Europe
Sales Price	$100.00	$102.00
Costs	80.00	82.00
Profit	$20.00	$20.00
	FairTax Pricing & Profit	
	U.S. Sales	Europe
Sales Price	$129.87	$102.00
Costs	80.00	82.00
FairTax	29.87	0.00
Profit	$20.00	$20.00

The first strategy for the manufactures post-FairTax would be to offer the product at the two different prices on the two continents and see what happens. At that point, the producer will have an incentive to walk the price up overseas to try to garner additional profits, seeing if the demand drops along the way. If the product has stopped selling in the U.S. because of the 30 percent price increase, there should be demand at least as great in the U.K. at the current price. If the higher prices in Europe produce with a per unit profit greater in the U.K. than the U.S., the most obvious incentive will be to spend more of the product marketing budget in the U.K. than in the U.S., to increase overseas sales at higher margins, and that's just the first of many down-stream effects. Wonderful news to all American companies that rely on the advertising budgets of American manufacturing businesses.

We also know that it would be profitable for an illegal operation to purchase the product in Europe and try to return it to the United States without paying the FairTax. The 30 percent differential would be an incredible incentive to try to avoid the FairTax by illegal, under the table sales. Certainly more than a few study-abroad Americans are going to pick up their Macs in London. And their iPhones. And their everything else.

We don't think the FairTax folks have a clue beyond their slogans of how such a massive price differential will impact American manu-facturing, but we go back to our political point: Any politicians advo-cating such a proposal is going to be skewered. Americans will simply find it unacceptable that foreigners can purchase American products for less than Americans.

Chapter 7

Imports

Everything imported will be subjected to a new 30 percent FairTax: South American lettuce during the winter, Scotch Whiskey All Year

Everything imported into the U.S. will ultimately get hit by the FairTax. Anything that is imported for direct sale or brought into the United States after being purchased abroad is supposed to be hit by the FairTax. Everything.

The ports and borders—already engines of efficiency—are going to become quite a bit more complicated to operate.

Current law provides that U.S. citizens are entitled to bring in a few hundred dollars of imported goods tax-free on their return from each trip abroad. (The amounts differ country by country and there are different time limits for the required period between trips with respect to certain countries.) The FairTax has an annual minimum amount of goods that can be brought into the United States tax-free. As will not surprise the reader at this point in the book, the rules for customs and the FairTax are not the same. The customs exemption is not calculated annually, but starts afresh with each new trip. What this means is that when a citizen returns from his second trip overseas, the purchases he or she brings back that would otherwise be exempt under the customs tax could well be taxable under the FairTax. But not necessarily. It depends on what was purchased and brought back earlier in the same calendar year. Sounds like a plan, right?

The only opportunity that the United States will have to assess the FairTax on certain goods will be upon entry of goods into the United States. The tax would thus have to be collected at the airport, port or Mexican and Canadian border prior to entry into the country.

Given the enormous sums of money at issue here—trillions of dollars of imports arrive each year—this is a huge expansion in the government tax collection establishment, and a huge incentive to cartel smuggling, which currently has its major profit incentive on outright banned substances. The FairTax will birth a generation of smugglers content to shoot for a 30 percent profit on anything it can slip past the nets, and given the flows of people in and out of the U.S., millions could join the trade in untaxed goods.

The other shoe that will fall with imports being subject to the FairTax is that obviously the cost of all imports will go up. That which is currently selling for x dollars will now cost an additional 30 percent. On the pricey side of life, the tag on that shiny European sports car will increase from $47,000 to more than $60,000. At the lower end, forget the imported cheese or French wine or the less expensive Chinese made sofa that the newlyweds were eying..

We acknowledge that the current trade rules need to be modified to give the United States an equal playing field with the World Trade organization, but the FairTax is not that reform, and taxpayers would be mortified by the higher cost of goods from overseas caused by the FairTax.

Chapter 8

Forcing The States To Tax More

S tates and all of their subdivisions—cities, utility districts, etc.—
must pay the FairTax on every good and service they purchase.

Non-federal government just got a bill for a 30 percent tax hike.

Start with the political calculation, again. Every single state and
local government official, employee and taxpayer is going to howl.
Then they are going to organize to punish the folks pushing this giant
new burden in their direction.

State and local governments cannot operate with a deficit. They
cannot print money. When their costs go up, taxes or borrowing must
increase on a dollar for dollar basis. The fiscal crises sweeping many
of the states as we prepare this book are because states are very poor
at saving money for rainy days. Their collective cupboards are bare,
some beyond bare and more than a few bankrupt by any conventional
definition.

The FairTax increases the cost of state and local government in
three direct manners.

First, as noted, state and local governments will be required to pay
the FairTax on all purchases of products for consumption, from pencils
to vehicles.

Second, the state and local government would be required to pay
the FairTax on virtually all salary costs –the salaries of educators get an
exemption in a rare if not exactly compelling nod to the political realities out there.

Finally, the <u>current</u> tax code provides state and local governments with a huge assist by allowing them to issue bonds, the interest on which is not taxable to the owner of the bonds. Under the FairTax the "tax-exempt" status of these bonds is destroyed, which will immediately cause interest rates paid by all states and cities on the monies they borrow to skyrocket.

This happens because bond purchasers no longer have an incentive—the tax savings under the current tax code—to buy the state and local bonds. To find buyers, the state and local governments will have to pay higher interest rates on the money they borrow, and the cost of those higher rates will be passed on to taxpayers.

The total U.S. state and municipal bond market approximates $2,600,000,000,000. (We love the visual impact of those zeros.). That amount is $2.6 trillion. State and local governments borrow such vast amounts of money because they do vast numbers of very expensive things, like building highways and bridges, universities and water purification plants.

Virtually every dollar of state and municipal debt is serviced at an interest rates a couple of points below those paid on bonds for corporate entities because of the tax-free nature of the state and local debt. If the interest rates on the existing bonds increased by 2 percent, this would have put an annual additional tax burden on state and local governments of $52 billion.

The increase in interest rates paid on public debt would be gradual as non-exempt bonds began replacing exempt bonds as the latter are redeemed, but there would be an immediate and enormous reduction in the value of these existing bonds as the FairTax would immediately reduce the value of these bonds as the non-taxable interest no longer has any special value. Indeed, it seems that all municipal bondholders would join the huge army of anti-utopians seeking to punish the party that brings forward such a destabilizing scheme.

These increased costs would require cities and states, already under significant and increasing financial pressure, to increase taxes. And the increases in taxes would be dramatic. The FairTax would cause the City of Charlotte and every other city in the country to pay the federal government a fee (the FairTax) if it chose to hire an additional police officer crossing guard, or social worker. The political ramifications of that conversation would prove interesting.

Charging the states for the FairTax is simply a ridiculous idea and subject to a constitutional challenge as discussed later. There is no intellectual justification for moving part of the cost of running the federal government to the states and simultaneously claiming lower tax rates at the federal level. We doubt that voters want the federal government to break the backs of the states in order to "simplify" the tax code.

A completely ridiculous FairTax payer is the federal government. The FairTax proposal requires the federal government to pay the FairTax itself on all of its purchases. If the federal government purchases a pencil or a tank, it pays itself the FairTax. This silliness might appear to be simply reaching in the left pocket for several hundred billion dollars and placing the funds in the right pocket, but this is not the case. The federal government would be paying two separate toll charges to collect its own money. The seller of the product receives a ¼ of 1 percent fee for collecting the tax and filing the appropriate forms and the State Sales Tax Administrating Authority receives an additional ¼ of 1 percent for collecting the tax. Therefore, for every billion dollars of expenses, the government adds an additional cost of $5,000,000 for the collection of its own funds. Taking this absurdity to the max, where the federal government becomes the State Sales Tax Administrating Authority because a state declines the opportunity to do so, this make work project would employ federal workers for the express purpose of collecting tax from itself to the tune of $2,500,000 per $1 billion dollars of purchases. Geniuses!

There is really no justification to charging either the federal or state governments federal taxes. In the case of the states, it is simply a movement of the deficit on to the backs of the states and in the case of the federal government, it is simply paying a collection fee to collect money it already has in the bank.

Chapter 9 –

Does Your Take Home Pay Go Up, Or Prices Down?

————— ⨎ —————

There is a little history between Hank and the most visible proponent of the FairTax, Neal Boortz, on the subject of embedded taxes and prices. It illustrates not just a difficulty in the scheme proposed by Neal, but also the difficulty in arguing with a moving target.

In late 2007, Hank wrote a piece for TownHall.com examining the FairTax. In the article, Hank chose to ignore a silly combination of claims advanced by Neal with respect to the FairTax. Hank thought he was doing Neal a favor, a gentlemanly sort of spotting Neal a couple of points.

The specific claims made by Neal Boortz in his first book on the subject, the *Fair Tax Book*, which Mr. Adler ignored were on behalf of the FairTax as follows:

1. *We start collecting 100 percent of our earnings in every paycheck.*
2. *We all get virtual raises, since payroll taxes are no longer siphoned from our checks.*
3. *The prices of consumer goods and services will remain essentially the same, with the removal of the embedded taxes compensating for the added consumption tax*

Hank ignored these claims because, in combination, they are impossible. The sum of the parts always equals the whole. Simply put:

If companies chose to pay the previously withheld income taxes and payroll taxes to the employees, those companies selling the products would be unable to reduce prices by that same amount. As a result, if costs remained the same and the FairTax was added to the sales price, prices couldn't remain essentially the same; prices must go up by the amount of the FairTax.

Neal still didn't seem to get it and responded in a column at TownHall.com:

> *"Here Adler once again ignores the role of embedded taxes. The price of consumer goods in this country would remain essentially the same. The embedded taxes are merely replaced by the FairTax."*

Perhaps Neal thought that an assertion, however wrong-headed, if repeated often enough would change the math. It doesn't.

Embedded taxes are defined by the FairTax proponents as taxes included in the price of consumer products purchased. A good example of embedded taxes would be that when a consumer purchases a cup of coffee, included in his purchase price are the income taxes withheld from the employees making and delivering the coffee along with the employee's share of federal payroll taxes and the employer's share of these payroll taxes.

With respect to the calculation of embedded taxes, the proponents of the FairTax rely on a study by Harvard's Dr. Dale Jorgenson. Dr. Jorgenson has determined that, on average, 22 percent of the price paid for a consumer product represents embedded taxes. The proponents of the FairTax provide a chart prepared by Dr. Jorgenson which indicates that prices would decline by 15 to 25 percent before the FairTax if embedded taxes were removed from the cost of all products. Neal Boortz further indicates that under Jorgenson's model, prices would drop an average of 29 percent over time as "even more taxes will be driven from the price". (Note: Dr. Jorgenson is not a supporter of the FairTax, and his study is not available for public review. Hank asked.)

Prices could indeed go down if embedded taxes are "driven" from the price of goods, but not if the employers of the workers making the goods keep the workers pay the same including their old withholding and the payroll taxes in their payroll checks, as promised by Neal.

Neal's "thinking" in this area is more than a little difficult to pin down, especially if you try and follow it across the various books and other writings. Neal must be aware of the key studies that predict an instant price hike of at least 30 percent on goods and services, but obviously doesn't believe them because in his latest book *FairTax: The Truth* Neal states in the introduction:

> *If the FairTax has one shortcoming, it's that it is easy to attack. Perhaps the most oft-repeated demagogic attack on the FairTax is that it "will add 23 percent to the cost of everything we buy." This, as you will learn is false. Because the FairTax is an "embedded " sales tax – that is, it is included in the price you pay, not added to the price – it will not increase the price of goods or services you buy. As we'll see, the retail prices you pay today already contain these embedded taxes; they're merely in a different form. The FairTax merely replaces one embedded tax with another."*

So it appears that Neal doesn't believe the studies. Fine.

However, in a chapter from *The FairTax: The Truth* entitled "Myths About the FairTax; It's Not A Miracle", Neal Boortz presents a multi-page discussion of prices where he discusses that in his travels, he has learned that taxpayers would prefer to have their take home pay increased rather than leave the embedded taxes with their employers. He then goes on to opine that that there will be a combination of price increase and decreases as the result of the FairTax. Finally, he concludes that:

> *So have we changed the equation? In the final analysis, not really. Reality warns us against promising a universal 22 percent reduction in retail prices. Remember, though, with that scenario you didn't get any increase in the pay you took home. It's become clear that we are going to see a combination of reduced prices and increased paychecks. In the final analysis, we're still dealing with the same fact: On average, 22 percent of the cost of every product or service you buy at the retail level represents the federal tax burden associated with bringing that product or service to the marketplace.*

That 22 percent would be taken out of the equation through a combination of price reductions and increases in the take-home pay of working Americans. Then the application of the 23 percent embedded FairTax would bring all of our purchasing power back to just about where we are right now. Any real increase in the price of goods and services would be offset by corresponding increases in the amount of money we take home from our jobs.

We are not sure that we or Mr. Boortz knows exactly where he stands on this issue at the moment.

We stand on math. You can't take the embedded taxes home in your paycheck and see prices fall. You cannot add a 30 percent sales tax and expect no one to notice.

And you can't keep changing your position without pointing out that your thinking is evolving as complexity invades the fantasy world of the FairTax.

We admire Neal's energy. Hugh has debated the FairTax with Neal in the East Room of the White House and in the Roosevelt Room outside of the Oval Office. Hank and Hugh applaud Neal's zest for the subject and his desire to make the tax system work, and we also applaud the attention he has brought to the subject of "embedded taxes."

But Neal's got to get real about the impacts of his risky scheme. (Remember when Al Gore used that phrase "risky scheme" unfairly against Jack Kemp in the vice-presidential debate of 1996? It's not unfair to use it to describe the FairTax scheme.) You can't take your payroll taxes home with you and believe the manufacturer is going to lower his prices by the amount of payroll taxes he isn't paying anymore, because he is only paying that same amount to his employees instead of the federal government.

Chapter 10

Bring A Calculator

—ॐ—

Under the FairTax regime, items would be priced and tax calcu-lated on a "tax-inclusive" basis. (Yes, that again.) The following is the way a retailer would determine his pricing and his final step before delivering each and every product to the shelves:

First Step: Determine how much money you want to receive from the transaction when it is over.

Second Step: Add all state and city sales taxes and excise taxes. State and city sales taxes and are calculated on a "tax-exclusive" basis. Excise taxes can be a tax-exclusive calculation or a stated amount. (Only the FairTax is calculated on a "tax-inclusive" basis.)

Step Three: Divide the sum of the first step and the second step by .77. That's the price to the public.

No, we aren't making this up. The FairTax folk will go a long way to use their "tax-inclusive" methodology to maintain the fiction that their tax rate is 23 percent.

Example: Assume you are a gasoline service station operator and you purchase a gallon of gasoline for $1.50 and intend to keep for yourself a $.15 profit on the sale of that gallon of gas.

Step One: You want to receive $1.65 for the gallon of gasoline from your customer.

Step Two: Let's assume the state and city local sales taxes are 10% and there is an excise taxes of 8 cents per gallon is in place. So, we add $.165 for the sales taxes (10% x $1.65) and 8 cents for the excise tax to get a pre-FairTax price of $1.895 ($1.65 + .165 + .08) per gallon.

Step three: We calculate the FairTax. To do this, we divide the $1.895 per gallon by .77 and we arrive at a price of $2.46 for our gallon of gasoline. (23 per cent of $2.46 is a $.565 FairTax per gallon which is the "tax-inclusive" calculation demanded by the FairTax proponents.)

Presto, there's your price. It looks like this on the receipt for one gallon of gas:

Price To Customer:	$2.460
FairTax (23%)	.565
State Sales Tax	.165
Existing Excise Tax	.080
Cost of a Gallon of Gasoline	1.500
Profit to the Gas Station Operator	.15

Repeat for every pack of chewing gum and every beef jerky you sell.

Oh, one more thing: The FairTax provides that the seller is required to inform the buyer and provide a receipt to the buyer which discloses the price without the FairTax, the FairTax paid, (and presumably other taxes paid), the total cost, the tax rate, the name of the vendor and the vendor registration number.

The gas station is actually among the least burdened of businesses. Wait until it is time to give a barber or a waitress a tip. Under the FairTax, that tip would be defined as part of the purchase price and the barber or waitress would be required to provide all of that information after applying the "tax-inclusive" formula to the transactions.

Again, sound like a thoroughly thought-through plan, eh?

Chapter 11

Tax Fraud, The Underground Economy and Overseas Banks

———— ∞∞∞ ————

If you have been to Manhattan in the past few years, you may have experienced a complete stranger wearing a knapsack walking up to you on a major street and asking if you want to buy some "smokes."

It has happened to both Hank and Hugh.

These gentlemen are providing the (illegal) opportunity to buy cigarettes without state and local taxes. New York State and New York City cigarette taxes total about $3.00 per pack. That hefty a tax is an incentive to fraud, and in fact ensures that fraud will be a certainty.

The street vendor of illegal smokes is obviously making more than minimum wage if he can move a couple of packs an hour. Add an additional $1.00 per pack FairTax on cigarettes, and the crooked seller of hot smokes of illegal cigarettes is looking at a 33 percent increase in his profits. The street vendor (and organized crime) applauds the highest FairTax rate possible.

There is ample academic research that tax fraud expands as sales tax rates go up. Tax fraud also logically expands as opportunities increase. Both are a concern under the FairTax. For states that abandoned their state income taxes following FairTax adoption, the combined federal, state and local sales tax rates could easily and significantly exceed 50 percent. This is sufficiently high for sales tax fraud to not just rise but to become rampant. Cash transactions will be the vehicle to fraud. The temptation to pay for any service with a price of $500 cash vs. $1000 with a credit card or check cannot be overlooked. Realistically, the buyer and the seller would pick a price in between $500 and $1000.

Neal Boortz in his "*The Fair Tax Book*" describes cash payments to "your maid, home repairman or house painter" as tax evasion under current law. And on this issue, he is completely correct. Neal identifies the Internal Revenue Service as indicating the loss from these actions costs the federal government $346 billion annually.

Neal also understands that these transactions will continue to evade taxation under the Fair Tax. But he underestimates how such frauds will explode both in volume and in size. One needs little imagination to consider the number of transactions that will not be reported under the Fair Tax. It is common sense to expect a massive expansion in tax fraud because the profit from it will increase dramatically and the enforcement forces arrayed against it will decline dramatically.

Fair Tax folks seem to believe that the Fair Tax collections will increase and fraud will decrease because when criminals buy food, houses, cars etc. they will have to pay the Fair Tax. This claim is featured in their literature. They believe that as the criminals will pay the Fair Tax upon legal purchases, this will create significant additional revenues. But the Fair Tax proponents badly miss on this issue as legal purchases by criminals (using their laundered money) are already taxed under the income tax laws. When Charlie the criminal makes a legal purchase today, the seller currently pays an income tax on the profit from the sale. There is little difference between the criminals' purchases of legal items under the current system vs. the Fair Tax.

Fair Tax proponents argue that under a Fair Tax, money would flood into the United States from Caribbean and other offshore banks. There is no question that foreign banks are sitting with illegal gains and profits as well as legal gains and profits from their customers which have avoided U.S. taxation and these amounts may easily be in the hundreds of billions. Fair Tax proponents don't seem to understand where the actual "cash" resides. Much of the money is already back in the United States as the result of direct and indirect loans from the foreign banks. Offshore banks do not keep their deposits in vaults under their offices. Like all banks, their profits come from lending the money to customers and paying the depositors interest with the difference resulting in their profit. This money that FairTax proponents believe would immediately flow back into the United States is all ready here.

In The "*Fair Tax Book*", in a chapter entitled "*Underground and Offshore Economy… Taxed at Last*" on page 104, after a tortuous discussion of how money came to be in offshore banks, Neal Boortz posits the following:

> *Remember, right now about $11 trillion in American wealth is sitting in banks and accounts in Europe, Asia, South America, the Caribbean, and elsewhere. This is money that is not working in the American economy. This is money that is not creating jobs and driving economic growth in our country. This is money that has fled our punishing tax structure, and would come flowing back if the income tax, both personal and corporate, were to be eliminated and replaced with a simple and fair consumption tax: the FairTax.*

So we ask, does anyone really think that the illegal drug money would flow back into the United States so that the Department of the Treasury could pounce on it as funds earned from illegal activity?

Next we turn to a different part of the underground economy. Under the FairTax, there is a Catch 22 for illegal residents operating business in the United States. There are thousands of these small businesses and they include auto mechanics, maids, landscapers etc. The FairTax requires registration of each of these businesses. However, if these businesses register under the FairTax regulations, there is some likelihood that a Social Security number would be required and a determination could follow that the owner of the business is illegal. If the law is then properly followed, deportation resulting. The incentive to stay underground and go "all cash, all the time" would be huge.

A final fraud nightmare is the impact of the FairTax on Social Security. Under current law, a worker must pay payroll taxes and an employer must pay matching payroll taxes. There is zero incentive under the current law to add non-working workers to an employer's payroll as that increases the tax bite to the employer. If there are no payroll taxes, there is all the incentive in the world to add all family members to a family business payroll and to the payroll information provided to the Social Security Administration. Unless the Social Security Administration dramatically increased staffing, there would be little opportunity for the Social Security Administration to review payrolls from businesses which include family members who actually performed no work, but who are now racking up benefit credits with no downside—payroll taxes—every family business in America will have an incentive to immediately "employ" all family members, and to recycle their "paychecks" into the business. The bottom line of the business stays the same, but each family members has increased their future claims on Social Security's resources.

Chapter 12

State Taxation After the Adoption of a Federal FairTax

———— ∞∞∞ ————

If the FairTax even draws near to adoption, the first issue for each state to consider is whether it should or could continue to administer its own income tax. In states that continued their income tax systems, to do this competently would require a significant expenditure of state tax revenues to replace the assistance currently provided by the IRS. In states which determined not to continue their state income tax systems, a new and effective tax system would have to be built. Where a state determined to increase its state sales taxes to collect the funds lost by their parallel decision to abandon income taxes, a decision would have to be made to adopt the FairTax methodology of collecting sales taxes (everything is taxed) and therefore abandon all of the current exemptions under state law or have its citizens faced with different FairTax and state sales tax regimens.

The alternative to uniform application is chaos: Sir, this item is taxable for the federal FairTax, not taxable for the state FairTax but yet taxable for the city FairTax."

Cities would face identical issues to the states, but with respect to the income tax imposed by many cities, it would be seemingly impossible to envision a city maintaining an income tax system where both the federal government and the state had closed up their income tax shops. These cities would have to move to a sales tax system.

How high do you think a combined federal, state and city FairTax rate would be?

An aside: In any state where the state income tax was left in place, their citizens would effectively lose all of the "time savings" benefits promised in the FairTax with respect to income tax preparation as the state would continue to require that process. The residents would be required to complete state individual and corporate tax returns nearly identical to the current federal income tax return along with acting to comply with the requirements of the federal FairTax.

The FairTax legislation anticipates that most states will effectively be forced to abandon their own tax regimens, with most moving to mirrors of the federal FairTax system. The draft legislation contains a section entitled: "Conforming State Sales Tax" where it defines the term *"conforming state sales tax to mean a sales tax imposed by a state that adopts the same definition of taxable property and services adopted by the FairTax."* (Cities with income taxes are not the subject of discussion in the draft legislation, where anything suggesting complexity is avoided.)

Thirty-eight states have state income taxes. Virtually every one of these states relies on the federal income tax system in some major part to administer their state income tax system. Virtually every state begins their individual state income tax form with "federal adjusted gross income" or "federal taxable income". Most states start their corporate tax returns with "federal taxable income." Virtually every state income tax code relies upon the Internal Revenue Code by reference or by replicating the federal Internal Revenue Code in defining the items essential to collecting an income tax. The definition of income is the same under every state income tax law as it is derived directly from the Internal Revenue Code. Most states refer directly and indirectly to the Internal Revenue Code and Regulations and the relevant case law to provide much, if not all of the legal underpinnings for their state law.

We aren't saying it isn't possible to unwind and rebuild the state tax codes, just that the FairTax folk haven't been exactly upfront in discussing how very, very complicated it will be. The FairTax folk have seemingly given no consideration to the costs of each state having to completely administer a state income tax system. They simply assume every state will choose to abandon their income tax systems.

Most states don't have the resources or the tax expertise to adequately review complex transactions, multi-state or multi-national corporations or complex tax returns. Their administrative income tax bureaucracies are designed to deal almost exclusively with state specific issues. Such state specific issues usually are found in the definition of residency for individuals, the proper allocation of income tax among the various states and the calculation of state-wide income. To continue a state income tax system under the FairTax, each state doing so would be required to administer their own income tax law without federal assistance. This would require the recreation of all of the elements of the federal courts and bureaucracy currently used to administer the federal tax system to administer their state tax. If all thirty-eight states maintained their own individual separate state tax systems, the current costs of law, regulation and audit may be multiplied by as much as thirty-eight times on a nationwide basis. Further, as time passes, each state would undoubtedly pass laws and rulings not consistent with other states and business and state courts would begin to adjudicate matters differently making the entire issue of complexity an entirely new matter for multi-state businesses. We won't bore you with the arcane area of Constitutional Law known as Dormant Commerce Clause jurisprudence, but it frowns on the destruction of the national marketplace via the multiplication of barriers to the free flow of goods and services. It does so because that free flow of goods and services was the prime mover behind the framing of the Constitution, and the national market it produced has yielded the dynamism that powered the growth of the U.S.

It is a very safe bet that even if the many state tax codes managed to avoid constitutional imperfection, after some period of time, the business compliance costs of operating a multi-state business would nevertheless be significantly higher under the FairTax than under present law. Over time as legislatures proposed and passed rules impacting their individual state income tax laws, there would be a growing difference between the old Internal Revenue Code and the individual state laws with respect to definitions and calculations.

This Balkanization of tax law would be a disaster for the economic vitality, a sort of wilful rush to embrace the morass of rules that Europe shed when it moved towards its economic union.

As we said the vast majority of individual and corporate audits conducted in the United States are conducted by the Internal Revenue Service. State taxing authorities tend to audit only for state residency and state specific income tax laws. This federal audit function is a very important element in keeping the cost of administering a state income tax system relatively low as most of the expense of auditing state income tax returns effectively resides with the Internal Revenue Service.

States also quite rationally rely on the deterrent effect of the looming IRS auditors to keep state taxpayers from cheating as well. In fact, all states with an income tax have arrangements with the Internal Revenue Service to share audit information, and individuals and corporations audited by the Internal Revenue Service generally receive a state billing at the end of the federal audit process. Most of the time, the company or individual never hears from the state except to receive a billing. Without the Internal Revenue Service, there would effectively be no meaningful income tax enforcement system in the United States, and each state would have to develop its own system, and pay for its operation.

The FairTax presents the individual states with the need to consider their own economic base vis-a-vis the FairTax system. The best example would be a farm state where a significant portion of the state revenues come from an income tax on successful farms and successful farmers. Little in the way of state FairTax revenues would be collected from those farmers as the crops would generally be consumed and the final consumption event by the individual buyer would occur in another state, so the repealed income tax revenue would not be made up unless the state's FairTax rate was exceptionally high. Some current taxpayers—say large corporate farming interests—could almost disappear from the state's tax rolls, with no way of replacing the lost state tax revenue.

Where some states would see a huge loss in tax revenues from repealed income taxes but no robust sales basis on which to recapture it, other states would face the nightmare of having to raise already staggeringly high sales tax rates in order to replace lost revenues from non-sales tax levies lost in the push towards a single tax system.

The FairTax proponents believe a federal FairTax rate of 30 percent (tax-exclusive) would be sufficient to produce in federal revenues equal all the federal taxes being repealed. William Gale of the Brookings

Institute believes that a FairTax rate of just under 50 percent (tax-exclusive) would be required assuming a 90 percent compliance element. There is no reliable research on the combined state and federal FairTax rates required to replace lost state revenues as states move towards parallel "sales tax only" systems, but they will have to be high when you consider how much revenue states take in.

Hypothetical rates simply do not put a face on the realities that America's vastly complicated economic landscape present. An example: New York state and New York City currently have a combined sales tax rate of 8.75 percent and an additional 9 percent plus hotel tax. Under the range of estimates, that would put the purchase of any item in New York City in a total sales tax rate of 38 percent to 58 percent (tax-exclusive). A hotel room would face a combines sales tax, hotel tax and FairTax rate of up to nearly 65 percent! And you thought hotels in the City were already expensive.

We cannot survey all 50 states, but the neither have the proponents made any attempt to provide a path forward that analyzes our federal system for what it truly is—50 different sovereign states that have each elected very different approaches to meeting their revenue needs based upon their unique economic and cultural circumstances. (There is but a single study which estimates individual state tax returns if the states adopt the FairTax methodology. Hank read the study and believes that there is a great deal more work to do before FairTax proponents can even begin to claim to know the impacts on state revenues and services from a FairTax regime.) Because the FairTax is a fantasy, state officials haven't spent much time bothering to point out the endless complexities that arise from the blunderbuss approach, and who can blame them given the fiscal crises enveloping their states?

If the FairTax proponents ever want to be taken seriously, they will produce not a pamphlet extolling the virtues of simplicity, but a book detailing the enormous complexities of the state-by-state transition plans they propose for guiding each of the states to the FairTax promised land. If you want to be a FairTax messiah in the 21st century, you should at least bring a map through the (extremely harsh) desert ahead.

Chapter 13

Gambling With Gaming—
An Illustration of The Trouble
With Simple Solutions

———⊗⊗⊗———

The FairTax folk purport to cover gambling in their scheme. Most Americans gamble to some degree—usually just a lottery ticket, an office pool, or a monthly poker game. And most Americans understand that large sectors of the economy are linked to gaming. You may be one of those Americans who disapprove, or a high roller with a suite waiting for you at Caesar's—no matter. What matters is that we all know that gaming is big business, and the FairTax's treatment of gaming will give us a good sense of how the simplicity of the scheme collides with the complexity of the economic realities of our vast American economy.

The bottom line: Taxing gaming income under a sales tax regimen is virtually impossible, but the FairTax folk try. The FairTax legislation gives us the following methodology for taxing "gaming":

A 23 percent tax is hereby imposed on the gaming services of a gaming sponsor. This tax shall be paid and remitted by the gaming sponsor.

The term gaming services means –

> *(1) Gross receipts of the gaming sponsor from the sale of chances, minus*
>
> *(2) The sum of (a) total gaming payoffs to chance purchasers (or their designees) and (B) gaming specific taxes (other than the tax imposed by this section) imposed by the federal, state or local government*

This proposal eliminates any possibility that the FairTax is "industry neutral" as its proponents claim. Gambling is obviously going to get hurt, big time. And the proposal demonstrates that there was not great care in considering what rate to apply to the gambling industry. There is no study of the gambling industry that produced a rate of tax on gross profits earned under gambling at 23 percent; it is simply the rate they charge on all FairTax items. It is not exactly random—it's a number designed to make a reader believe that the FairTax is being applied equitably to all businesses. Frankly, any proposed tax rate except 23 percent would have demonstrated some thought was given to the issue.

But it's not. The tax proposed is not on the gamblers and their winnings. The gamblers who are consuming the services of the casino are not paying the sales tax that all other consumers of all other goods and services are paying. This 23 percent tax is a tax on a specific business, one for which the collection of a sales tax is virtually impossible. A quick look at the books of many public companies in the gambling business would indicate that the costs of operating a casino are very, very significant, and it would go up dramatically under the FairTax.

Many, if not most casinos, would lose money if subjected to this new 23 percent tax on net receipts. Forget all of those jobs in Nevada, New Jersey, Louisiana and tribal reservations everywhere. And forget all of those state gambling tax revenues. And forget the monies that most state lotteries give to schools. California earns about $1.152 billion a year on their lottery; with a FairTax it is reduced to $795 million.

FairTax folk are in love with simplicity, and the appeal of their movement is deeply anchored in our collective desire to make smooth the rough spots, and to level the mountains of paper associated with our current tax code.

But ask yourselves how many other industries are there that, like gaming, just don't fit well under the mirage of the FairTax? How many other industries are going to get a note: "Sorry, your operations are too complicated for us. Send us 23 percent (or 30 percent or 50 percent) of your revenues."

You may not approve of gambling, but at least thank the people of Vegas for casting a bright light on the Fair Tax's gaps.

Chapter 14

Revenue Neutral? Really?

— ∞∞∞ —

The FairTax has triggered a lot of debate about taxes in general and that's good.

It has also stoked a lot of conversation about tax reform. That's even better.

Best of all, it has forced people to focus on the staggering amount of money the federal government collects through its web of taxes. This vast pile of extracted money is too often overlooked because it accumulates unseen from a variety of sources.

The FairTax proponents want to wipe out all federal taxes except the FairTax, and to keep the debate simple, they say the FairTax rate should be set at that rate that will replace all current federal tax revenues. They claim that the Fair Tax will be "revenue neutral."

There is great debate with respect to whether the revenue produced by a FairTax rate of 30 percent is sufficient to equal the taxes collected from the current federal individual and corporate income taxes, payroll taxes and estate and gift taxes. The one thing that appears certain is that none of the models that have been prepared take into consideration changes in behavior from a change to a FairTax.

Almost all of the economic models which the authors have been able to find (and there are very few studies) presume 100 percent compliance with the law when it comes to calculating revenue neutrality. This is of course wishful thinking. A study by William Gale of the Brookings Institute indicates that the FairTax rate would need to be increased by twenty percentage points if compliance were at 80 percent (a reasonable but still optimistic compliance rate in our view) instead of 100 percent. (BTW: In Gale's model, this level of compliance increases the required FairTax rate from the 40 percent he thinks is needed at 100 percent compliance to a 60 percent FairTax, before including state taxes.)

There are four economic studies that are useful when considering "revenue neutrality.". The President's Advisory Panel of Tax reform concluded that it would take a 34 percent "tax exclusive" tax rate under the FairTax to equal *only* the amount of funds collected from the federal income tax and to pay the Prebate. While they do not quantify the FairTax rate that would be needed to include payroll taxes and estate taxes, the Panel's study would seem to forecast a total necessary FairTax rate approaching 50 percent for all federal taxes to be replaced.

As noted above, William Gale of the Brookings Institute calculates that the necessary FairTax rate with 100 percent compliance would approximate 41 percent using a "tax-exclusive" rate and a 60 percent rate with 80 percent compliance. Dr, Gale's study points out the high cost of non-compliance by taxpayers under a FairTax regime.

A study released by the Beacon Hill Institute indicates that a 31.27 percent FairTax rate is required to replace the federal revenue sources eliminated. The Beacon Hill Institute study does not appear to consider non-compliance.

The Arduin, Laffer & Moore Econometrics Group also calculates a rate of "30 percent tax- exclusive," but this study also concludes that a "small" spending cut would be necessary to make the 30 percent rate work, which of course means it isn't a revenue neutral rate. This study also does not appear to consider a lack of 100 percent compliance within the system.

Against this evidence, the 30 percent rate just isn't persuasive. Debating an artificially low rate is spin of the worst sort.

Chapter 15

The Complications of The Constitution and Treaties

—◈◈◈—

Most FairTax proponents assume that moving to a FairTax will require repeal of the 16th Amendment to the Constitution, which is itself an Amendment to the Constitution. We are tempted to say, "Fine. Call us when you get the measure before the states."

Many FairTax proponents insist on the repeal of the 16th Amendment to the Constitution before enactment of a FairTax because they believe that without the repeal of the federal income tax, which was the result of the 16th Amendment, they would face either the probability or possibility of having both the FairTax federal sales tax and a federal income tax. This is a reasonable fear, but getting such an amendment passed is an unreasonable "assumption."

Proposed amendments to the Constitution are a dime a dozen. Nothing is easier for a member of Congress to do than propose an amendment to the Constitution of the United States.

The last amendment to get approved was an obscure measure dealing with Congressional pay that made it through the long obstacle course in 1992. Prior to that, it was 1971, with the amendment that dropped the voting age to 18—not exactly a controversial measure either.

Most experts doubt very much whether any complicated amendment will ever again successfully sail the waters of the long course to ratification. The D.C. statehood amendment failed in 1986 as did the

Equal Rights Amendment a few years earlier. Americans are very, very leery of messing with the Framers' work.

FairTax proponents may respond that this is just why activism is needed. Perhaps. Practical politics tells us that the here and now requires leaders focused on the next few years while the movement for tax reform grows. Thus any candidate who is campaigning on the FairTax is campaigning on a platform he or she cannot possibly hope to see implemented within the next decade. That's observation number one.

Observation number two is that any proposed FairTax amendment would have to be thoroughly considered opposite all other Constitutional guarantees and international agreements. Simple repeal of the 16th Amendment would in no way guarantee that the FairTax would survive scrutiny under our system of dual sovereignty guaranteed by the Tenth Amendment. There is a huge coercive effect in the proposed FairTax on the states, and one or more of them will surely argue that as a separate sovereign, it cannot be made to wholly rewrite its tax laws as a result of the Congressional imposition of the FairTax, and others will argue that it is simply unconstitutional for the federal government to tax state purchases in the first place. FairTax proponents will reply that no coercion is required by the FairTax scheme, but federal courts dig deep into such arguments and have a genuine concern that the states remain the free and independent sovereigns they are intended to be.

There are a many other constitutional issues raised by the FairTax, including the exclusion of illegal aliens from the Prebate. If the courts rule that such a policy is unconstitutional, the entire FairTax scheme is upended. Because of the complexity of the new scheme, it would be Constitutional roulette to rely upon the validity of a FairTax statute as opposed to a FairTax Amendment spelling out the details of the scheme. Mere repeal of the 16th Amendment won't cut it.

There are also numerous issues connected with the international obligations of the United States undertaken by treaty. There is no short cut out of our treaty obligations, no right for the U.S. to simply declare the old game—and international order—over and a new one commenced with radical new rules and radical new prices attached to U.S. exports. In an interconnected, global economy, the prospect of the U.S. simply legislating an entirely new approach to pricing and taxation without long consultation with friends and foes alike is just another fantasy.

Like the prospect of repealing the 16th Amendment.

Chapter 16

Legal Residents and Illegal Immigration

———— ∞∞∞ ————

The Prebate is proposed to be paid only to lawful residents with Social Security numbers. This definition would include both citizens and non-citizens. The Prebate would go to all green card holders and the children of illegal residents who were born in the United States and are thus U.S. citizens. It would include all foreign college students studying in the United States. It would include the ambassadors and United Nations workers from North Korea, Iran and Venezuela living in New York City if they obtain Social Security numbers .

There are some interesting possibilities with respect to the Prebate and legal and illegal immigrants.

At least 12 million and as many as 25 million men, women and children who are illegal immigrants would not be eligible for the monthly Prebate. One question that needs to be asked is: What would happen on the Monday morning that prices increased by a minimum of thirty percent and one hundred percent of illegal immigrants received nothing while every other resident of the United States was beginning to receive a monthly Prebate?

In cities with significant illegal populations there is the obvious possibility of peaceful civil disobedience. Or worse. These are large populations, and they will believe that they have been specifically and shamefully victimized by a large price hike on life's necessities. They will not be eager to see their families miss an occasional meal with the new pricing. Many of the illegal immigrants with perfectly legal children would have been afraid to apply for a prebate for their children less they be rushed out of the United States.

Any system that proposes to send a monthly check to every foreign student enrolled at every American university but which refuses to send that check to any illegal alien no matter how many years they have been resident in the county or how many legal children they have is absurdly generous and absurdly provocative at the same time.

Chapter 17

Tax Planning For a FairTax

———— ∞ ————

"Anyone may arrange his affairs so that his taxes shall be as low as possible; he is not bound to choose that pattern which best pays the treasury. There is not even a patriotic duty to increase one's taxes. Over and over again the Courts have said that there is nothing sinister in so arranging affairs as to keep taxes as low as possible. Everyone does it, rich and poor alike and all do right, for nobody owes any public duty to pay more than the law demands."

Judge Learned Hand

Hank worked for four decades as an accountant with one of the country's largest public accounting firms, where a great deal of time, money and skill is expended to legally minimize taxes for individuals and corporations. Citizens rightly and legally attempt to reduce their taxes to the lowest legal amount.

And they will continue to do so, even as the FairTax debate unfolds, and especially if the FairTax fantasy ever approached reality.

What would happen on the eve of the FairTax? Both individuals and corporations would, of course, do everything in their power to reduce income taxes in the last year of the income tax under the

Internal Revenue Code and reduce the FairTax under the first year of the FairTax. This perfectly legal exercise would cost the Treasury billions, maybe hundreds of billions.

Tax planners would be attracted to the final income tax year like bees to flowers. Their last dance with the Internal Revenue Code. Their first dance with the FairTax.

What would individuals do? Everything they could to show losses in their personal tax returns and reduce their final year income tax to nothing. Individuals would attempt to complete purchases in the final year as well. Car and house purchases would skyrocket as never before, though pricing of the latter would be difficult to predict given the turbulence of the housing market that would follow.

Some individuals would simply not file tax returns and rely on the short fuse included in the FairTax legislation for the end of the Internal Revenue Service. Fraud would be rampant including non-filing fraud, exclusion of taxable income and inclusion of bogus deductions. The fraud-minded would sense that the imminent collapse of the IRS would cover a multitude of sins.

Every individual taxpayer in the United States would be attempting to do the maximum personal tax planning possible in the final year of the federal income tax. Such efforts would include completely legitimate actions such as:

- Prepayment of state and property taxes creating maximum deductions in the final year – Only a fool would not get every penny of that state tax deduction into the last year of the income tax as the deduction would be worthless in the next year
- Prepayment of contributions for the next year – To the extent a taxpayer annually makes charitable donations, making donations for the succeeding year would drive taxes down with the reality that in future years, all contributions would be with after-tax dollars.
- Wealthier taxpayers would place future contributions into entities where they would be tax deductible today and the actual contributions could be made in later years—This is perfectly legal and deductible under the current Internal Revenue Code.

- Prepayment of medical expenses and payment of old medical expenses. Taxpayers would insure that every dollar possible was taken as a tax deduction in the last year of the income tax.

- Sale of all assets which could produce an ordinary loss and all assets to the extent of other gains to create a maximum capital loss of $3000.

- There are rules under the Internal Revenue Code which make it impossible to repurchase these items within 30 days after sale and take the loss, but with the demise of both the Internal Revenue Service and a next year income tax return, at best, it would almost impossible to track the subsequent year purchases.

- Deferral of all sales of property where there would be a taxable gain. Anyone contemplating the sale of any property at a gain (including securities) would, if at all possible, wait until the federal income tax was eliminated before executing the transaction.

- Transactions where the purchase would occur for the purchaser and the income would be deferred for the seller would be the item of the day.

- Deferral of salary and other income through the use of any device possible including "Rabbi trusts," late payments of bonuses etc. Whatever could be done to move income from the final year of the Internal Revenue Code to the first year of the FairTax would take place.

- Maximization of depreciation methods.

- One particularly elegant tax planning device would be the legal payment to a self employed retirement plan. This payment is due on April 15th, at the time of filing the personal tax return. A taxpayer in the 34 percent tax bracket could make this payment, a maximum of $40,000 on April 15th and reduce his or her taxes by $13,600. On April 16th, that person could retrieve the money from their retirement plan tax-free.

What tax planning would occur the day after the FairTax?

- Any taxpayer with a wit of sense would eliminate all deferred assets and create transactions to insure that the income taxability of such transactions took place as soon as possible after the implementation of the FairTax and the income taxation was zero. This would be done to offset any possibility that the income tax would be reinstated and taxes would be collected in the future.

Corporations would also change their behavior.

- There are special rules for inventories in the first year of the FairTax and these would cause every corporation or business to build extreme levels of inventory before the FairTax was put into place. Here alone there are billions of dollars to be saved by having completed inventory in place for the first year of the FairTax.
- Corporations would defer their dividends to avoid the income tax for their shareholders in the final year of the Internal Revenue Code. Indeed, if is the FairTax moved towards reality, such deferrals—and their impact on individuals depending on them—would become routine.

This is just a partial list, and the nation's legions of CPAs and tax lawyers would get to work on far more intricate schemes. The FairTax folk will note that this is a two-year transition phenomenon that will pass, and perhaps that is true, but the massive incentives to act on the approach of such a massive change promises the wildest economic ride in modern times, greater even than the dislocations of 2008 and 2009, raising the question of whether the country as a whole wants a roller coaster with that large a loop—especially one that's never been ridden before.

Chapter 18

FairTax Claims:
The Moving Targets

—❦—

O ne of the most interesting aspects of the promotion of the FairTax has been the on-going "clarification" and/or "abandonment" of the original and very central claim of the scheme's sponsors with respect to the FairTax without making a complete and amplified retraction.

In moving from *The FairTax Book* in hardback to the *FairTax Book* in paperback, the silliest and yet, perhaps most important claim of the FairTax proponents disappeared. We discuss this claim several times in this book because it was initially one of the cornerstones of the FairTax movement and because it was and is so clearly wrong.

The claim in the Hardback edition of *The FairTax Book*:

1   *We start collecting 100 percent of our earnings in every paycheck*
2   *We all get virtual raises, since payroll taxes are no longer siphoned from our checks*
3   *The prices of consumer goods and services will remain essentially the same, with the removal of the embedded taxes compensating for the added consumption tax*

Fairly obviously, if our withholding and payroll taxes, which are embedded taxes, are no longer paid to the federal government and are paid directly to us, there will be no removal of any costs to the employer-producer as the employee-producer now pays these taxes directly to the employee. If, on the other hand, the withholding and payroll taxes are kept by the company and the prices of goods and services lowered prior to the imposition of the sales tax, there would be no "100 percent" of our earnings and no virtual raises. Hence, the preposterous "win-win" promise could not possibly be kept.

The claim in the paperback edition of *The Fair Tax Book*:

1 *We start controlling our earnings in every paycheck*
2 *Our purchasing power for buying consumer goods and services remains essentially the same, with the removal of the embedded taxes compensating for the added consumption tax.*

The change in this claim was not mentioned in the paperback edition of *The Fair Tax Book*, not in the *Preface*, not in the *Introduction*, not in the *A Word from Congressman John Linder* or *A Word from Neal Boortz*.

As discussed earlier, the book *Fair Tax: The Truth* has what appear to be multiple answers to this question, but none of the economists who have studied the issue have concluded that the original claim could be kept.

This claim of increasing wages and decreasing prices remains central in many of the arguments in the public domain and has created a level of misinformation that represents a very serious barrier to a reasonable discussion of the Fair Tax.

The truth: Prices are going to go up on many key goods and services and some employers will pocket payroll taxes they are no longer paying. There is simply no way to predict the millions and millions of pricing decisions that would follow such a revolution in taxation.

Chapter 19

To Repeat: We Want Tax Reform, Just Not Blunderbuss Fantasy Reform

———— ∞∞∞ ————

We think the tax laws of the federal government need major reform. You can't have spent your entire professional life in close contact with the system as Hank has and not know just how extraordinarily costly and ugly the system is. There are indeed some relatively precise changes that could be made to the current income tax system that would dramatically increase simplicity without undoing a system that still generally works to produce the revenues the government needs. These changes, though simple, would be significant in that they would reduce the level of tax preparation difficulty for millions of Americans.

Life is not simple, however, and neither is business. In fact, the processes of business and its complexity in today's world rival any complexity found in rocket science. This creates the dilemma of either having an Internal Revenue Code that is too complex for the average person to understand and too complex for that taxpayer to prepare his own tax return or of having an Internal Revenue Code which is insufficiently complex and allows large businesses and wealthy taxpayers to take actions which avoid their paying their "fair share" of the funds necessary to operate the country. Today, the Internal Revenue Code is designed to protect the flow of federal revenue and is therefore extremely complicated.

That being said, the Internal Revenue Code complexity could be significantly reduced for the average taxpayer if the various rates were removed from the Code and some basic elements of the Code were modified.

Former Arkansas governor and once-and-future presidential candidate Mike Huckabee is a vocal backer of the FairTax. His support of the FairTax undoubtedly led to some of his early success in the 2008 GOP primaries. In his recent book, "*Do the Right Thing*," Governor Huckabee includes a chapter about the FairTax entitled "*The Fairness and Force of the FairTax*". In this chapter, Mr. Huckabee addresses the issue of hidden taxes by stating:

> *The current tax system is pretty sneaky. Congress has designed it so that most Americans don't really see how much they pay in taxes each year. That's one of the real injustices of our tax system; so much of what we pay is hidden from us.*

We agree with Governor Huckabee: The lack of transparency as to many of the taxes Americans pay is a serious issue. One of the important issues that the FairTax debate has brought to center stage is the level and mass of federal taxes being paid in the United States and their lack of visibility in total. But this argument isn't new—Ronald Reagan used this argument to advance his policies routinely—and the argument isn't "owned" by FairTax proponents.

Governor Huckabee also wrote

> "*The tax system in our nation is broken. Badly broken. Worse than that, it is beyond repair.*"

This is just wrong. It is like saying that every car involved in a crash needs to be "totaled," when in fact most just need repair. The only barrier between the current Internal Revenue Code and a much better Internal Revenue Code is the same Congress that would need to address the FairTax. It is simply a question of Congress having the backbone, to use Mr. Huckabee's book title, to "*Do the Right Thing*".

Congress should fix the Internal Revenue Code. They should make it a priority and they should do it now. Significant "reform" is needed, but not the scheme advanced by the FairTax. Our biggest problem with the FairTax fantasy is that it drains energy and attention from the problem at hand, sucking oxygen from the necessary debate about what can and should—and crucially—***could*** be done right now, even with Democratic majorities in both houses of Congress and a Democratic president.

Chapter 20

Claims You Can Rely On Not

— ∞∞∞ —

Fair Tax proponents have not been shy in advancing very impressive claims on behalf of the FairTax. Here's the list taken from the FairTax.org. website's suggested talking points for proponents of the FairTax as of early 2009, as well as a couple of claims put forward by Governor Huckabee. The claims are in italics, and our comments follow.

- *Allows you to keep 100 percent of your paycheck, pension, and Social Security payments.*

This is rhetorical sleight-of-hand. Most people do not work in order to "keep our paycheck." Rather, most people work to earn money to buy things and accumulate savings. The core issue in the tax reform debate is not how much we initially receive in a paycheck. The issue is how much wealth we can accumulate while purchasing the goods and services we need and want. Thus the "paycheck" claim is effectively a meaningless claim—a rhetorical flourish. If the FairTax causes prices on essentials to rise so dramatically that wage earners are impoverished, keeping 100 percent of a paycheck won't matter as it quickly goes out the door and fewer goods, services and savings come back in.

- *Frees up the time wasted on filling out complicated IRS forms.*

The FairTax would indeed eliminate the preparation of the federal income tax return for the Internal Revenue Service. But for the self-employed, the FairTax will require a replica of Schedule C from the current federal income tax return in order to calculate "taxable income" for purposes of receiving benefits from the Social Security Administration. It is the complexity of determining income which makes the Internal Revenue Code complicated and all of this complexity will manifest itself in the new filing for the Social Security. Administration required by the FairTax.

Instead of a federal income tax return, each family will have to annually register their family with the State Sales Tax Administrating Authority for the state in which they reside. For many families, this process and the family size and address changes may prove more daunting than a Form 1040 A. Those who currently don't file an income tax form because they lack income will now have to file forms with the government. Today, single taxpayers earning under $8,950 and married couples earning under $17,900 a year do not need to file federal income tax returns. And if we are honest about it, the filing of a 1040A should not take more than an hour.

If the state in which the taxpayer resides continues to have a state income tax, the taxpayer will need to continue to prepare annual income tax returns requiring calculations identical or nearly identical to their current federal income tax returns.

And any household which employs a domestic servant or gardener will have to pay the FairTax and file the appropriate forms therewith.

(One note that many will disagree with is that the preparation of the annual tax return may not be such a bad thing in any event. The requirement forces a large percentage of Americans to annually asses their financial situation and to annually have a peak at their total income tax and payroll tax liabilities. The payment of FairTax at every transaction will not provide the taxpayer with an annual look at the amount of taxes being paid in total.)

- *Wipes out the income tax code and shuts down the IRS.*

The FairTax replaces the Internal Revenue Service with up to fifty separate state Sales Tax Administrating Authorities, a new organization within the federal Treasury Department and a bloated Social Security Administration. (The Treasury will have to create a new agency to administer the laws of the FairTax.)

The proposed elimination of the Internal Revenue Service is so precipitous that during the implementation of the FairTax, tax compliance and audits from the last two or three years of the federal income tax will be so significantly reduced that it is likely that the Treasury will bleed billions.

The FairTax simply cannot completely eliminate the Internal Revenue Code. It would remain in part for the calculation of Social Security benefits for the self employed and will be used to provide guidance for the FairTax.

- *Makes taxation of income unconstitutional by repealing the 16ᵗʰ Amendment through companion legislation.*

The proposed FairTax law does not repeal the 16ᵗʰ amendment. This would take a constitutional amendment which is a far more major undertaking than the passing of the FairTax. Minimizing the near-impossibility of this amending process takes the entire discussion of the FairTax and puts it in the land of fantasy.

- *Exempts all taxpayers from federal taxation up to the poverty level, through a monthly rebate.*

This comment is factually incorrect, which may be shocking to some FairTax proponents. As discussed earlier, it appears that the drafters of the FairTax became a bit confused by the use of the tax-inclusive methodology. If the FairTax exempted all taxpayers from federal taxation to the poverty level, the Prebate would need to be calculated at 30 percent of the poverty level expenditures instead of the 23 percent in the legislation

- *Ensures that all Americans pay their fair share of taxes.*

This claim is simply silly. There is no tax system where everyone will pay their "fair share" because there is no definition of "fair share" with which everyone or even most people concur. Whether the American public would accept and find "fair" that an American receiving $100,000,000 of interest and dividends could pay virtually no FairTax (the possibility of which is indisputable) is very much in doubt.

This ridiculous claim also avoids discussion of the criminal element that will always and everywhere seek to defraud the government, forcing on to honest citizens the cost of shouldering their share of taxes.

- *Dramatically lowers tax rates for low-income and middle-income Americans.*

The conclusions of the President's Advisory Panel on Federal Tax Reform and many other studies state that this claim is false.

- *Makes taxes visible by eliminating hidden income and payroll taxes in consumer prices.*

If retailers comply with the requirement of showing the taxes included in the price of every item, this claim is correct. See our earlier discussion of the enormous costs this imposes on retailers. And note, the FairTax is death by a thousand cuts as while one <u>might</u> see the tax on each transaction , the total of taxes paid through the year will become invisible to all but the most vigilant and organized.

- *Enables families to save more for home ownership, education, and retirement.*

If federal tax revenues are going to remain the same as the FairTax folks claim, this is an absurd argument. Someone has to pay those taxes. It will certainly be true that some families will have more after-tax income; it is equally true that some families will have less after-tax income. We are certain that almost all wealthy families will be celebrating the day the FairTax is enacted.

- *Protects and ensures the funding of Social Security and Medicare.*

The government is already committed to funding Social Security and Medicare and can by legislation change that commitment. There is nothing in any bill passed by Congress and signed by the President that in future years cannot be changed the next day or the next month by that same Congress and President or the next Congress and President. The FairTax would be subject to change or repeal on day one, just like any other law passed by Congress and signed by the President of the United States. This is just meaningless, but deeply misleading rhetoric.

- *Leaves unchanged the amount of money raised by the federal government.*

There is great uncertainty as to how much the FairTax will collect. Many studies dispute the claims made by the FairTax proponents.

- *Makes American products more competitive overseas.*

This claim is more hocus-pocus and understates the enormous complexity of the shift proposed and the trade retaliation it is likely to trigger.

- *You never pay another hidden tax again. The FairTax is printed on every receipt for every purchase.*

As though every American looks at every receipt to begin with, but even if they do, the nightmare for retailers and their pricing policies using the "tax inclusive" methodology is just beginning.

- *All taxpayers are treated fairly. No loopholes for anyone.*

In the Internal Revenue Code, one person's "loophole," is another person's definition of fairness. Both the deduction for home interest and medical expenses can be loopholes for one and intelligent social incentives for another. As people become knowledgeable about FairTax, tax planning strategies will develop and new loopholes will be identified.

- *Individuals have more control and choice. People can make choices about how much to pay in taxes, by deciding when to buy and what to buy.*

Taxpayers today can control the amount of income taxes they pay by their investment decisions and how much they work. In some ways, the FairTax provides far less individual control as taxpayers cannot determine not to eat or to skip urgently needed medical care. For many Americans, the tax choices become fewer not greater under the FairTax.

- *Virtually all economic models project a much healthier economy under the FairTax. Real investment will grow by an estimated 76.4 percent. Exports will jump by an estimated 26.4 percent. Interest rates will drop between 20 and 30 percent.*

Ignoring the short run versus the long run, we find this claim absurdly certain given the enormous uncertainties connected with transition to a radical new system. Maybe it will work out. Proponents of the FairTax are free to make outlandish claims, but treating them as debating points is ridiculous. The FairTax precision of projecting exact growth rates is a high school debate trick.

- *Small businesses never have to track tax withholdings or deductions.*

The FairTax would eliminate federal withholding, the most effective manner of tax collection in the world, but also the most resented. This is the great emotional appeal of the FairTax—keeping all of what we earn from work. But at the moment of the FairTax's adoption, vast new taxes become payable, prices rise, and new State Sales Tax Administrating Authorities spring into being to collect taxes (and harass the businesses that are obliged to collect the FairTax and its state counterparts.)

State withholding and income taxes are not guaranteed to vanish and if a state does not eliminate their income tax, the promised benefits of simplicity are greatly diminished if not completely destroyed. No ideas have been presented to deal with state disability withholding and the other routine deductions such as medical premiums. Also vanishing: Tax-preferred savings for retirement. Will you and all those you know move to the disciplined savings encouraged by our current tax code?

Replacing federal withholding with reporting to the Social Security Administration follows for business and the self-employed under the FairTax. While there is no withholding, the new paperwork could be significant.

The promises to small businesses of great simplicity are overstated. The Social Security Administration will require a calculation of taxable income (a bit modified), and small business will be required to keep track of its deductions. Lots of auditing is guaranteed, because lots of cheaters will still be with us.

In fact, there are plenty of record keeping responsibilities under the FairTax, and to the extent the record keeping is insufficient to implement the law, we can count on statutory language to increase that record keeping.

- *Tax evasion dramatically decreases. No more income reporting means the end of "hiding" income from tax authorities.*

We await the drug cartels' first payment of their FairTax. Studies show that increases in sales tax rates lead to increased tax fraud. Many believe that a very high sales tax will result in very, very substantial "hiding" of transactions.

- *Compliance costs are slashed. Compliance costs drop by over 90 percent, from $265 billion.*

The claim of $265 billion of tax preparation cost is without wide support. When one tries to value the time of an individual preparing a tax return, it gets very little silly in a hurry, especially when tax preparation time is replaced with a nap.. The costs of tax compliance are certainly significant, but the FairTax folk cook this stuff up and serve it without any serious discussion.

We worry some –not much, but some—about the impact of the FairTax on accounting firms and associated service industries. There certainly will be some victims with respect to the myriad of individuals who prepare tax returns every spring to make their worlds work, and of course whole university departments are built on the complexity of the IRS tax code. The complexities associated with the "simple" FairTax are huge enough, however, to create new opportunities for the small-print minded and those who train them..

Mike Huckabee's Claims

In Governor Huckabee's book *Do the Right Thing*, he makes a few comments and claims with respect to the FairTax:

> *The economists who helped create the FairTax estimated that the people in the top one-third of the economy would benefit by 4 percent or 5 percent under the FairTax; those in the middle would benefit by 7 percent to 8 percent by implementing the FairTax; and those in the bottom third of the economy could actually benefit by as much as 12 percent because of a disproportionate amount of their income paying income and payroll taxes versus taxes on the new items at the retail level.*

Right. Never has so much been promised with so little data (or qualification) provided. If the federal government is collecting the same amount of tax after passage of the FairTax, it is a bit hard for each third of the economy to benefit. There is no fourth third to provide all that new revenue to the other thirds.

The FairTax would virtually eliminate the underground economy

Many who have studied this issue are convinced that the rate of compliance with the FairTax would be no better and perhaps far worse than the current system. Certainly, no one should be predicting that the underground economy will be virtually eliminated.

If we eliminated the IRS, we would cut a $10 billion-a-year government program.

The $10 billion dollar a year program could well be replaced with at least a $20 billion dollar a year program with hundreds of billions of dollars in start-up costs as the federal government and 50 states struggle to "simplify". Further, the promised payments to the State Sales Tax Administrating Authority and the companies preparing sales tax forms will equal more than the $10 billion currently being spent for the IRS. Add to this the cost of increasing the size and scope of the Social Security Administration and the government will spend considerably more collecting the same revenues they currently collect with the IRS.

Political rhetoric is a wonderful thing, especially when advanced in connection to a proposal that has zero chance of success and thus generates very little in the way of serious study by other than its proponents.

Ask yourself, if the FairTax was this great, why hasn't every candidate on the GOP side been advancing it for years?

Answer: It is an anvil around the neck of any serious candidate if and when it was put forward in a general election campaign for all the reasons discussed in this book.

The FairTax is a slogan supported by slogans, a wonderful talking point for some talk show hosts, and political poison for any serious candidate who faces serious questions over a sustained period of time by informed critics.

Prediction: If the talented Governor Huckabee ever gets close to the GOP nomination, his advocacy of the FairTax will slowly and then quickly evolve into a much more general—and defensible—call for tax reform and relief. Either that, or he and the GOP gets hammered in the year he tops the ticket for all the reasons outlined in this book but amplified by a hostile mainstream media.

You read it here first.

Chapter 21

Thinking Like A State

—∞∞∞—

The FairTax is built on the assumption that the states will go along with the revolution and applaud the sweeping away of the old and its replacement with the new. The FairTax folk have provided against the contingency of a state here or there saying "No thanks," but generally the expectation is that sooner or later the states will throw into the sales tax game.

We don't think so. In fact, we think the states will organize very effectively to block the FairTax were it to ever develop any serious momentum in Congress whether towards H.R. 25 or towards any amendments repealing the 16th Amendment and creating the FairTax.

There are numerous reasons why the states—as represented by their state elected and appointed officials—will hate the FairTax. We'll stick with the big three: sovereignty, stability and administrative costs.

First, states really do care about their sovereignty. The uniqueness of our American system of government is rooted in the dual sovereignty of state and federal government, and states have always acted to protect as much of their independence as they can preserve against the steady encroachment of the feds.

Freedom-loving people should applaud this as competition for authority between the two sovereigns leads to a division of power between them, which means less total government power over individuals.

It is certainly true that two tax systems are more expensive than one, but extra expense is a cost long associated with liberty, and one most Americans have been willing to pay.

Say goodbye to genuine state sovereignty once the federal government can charge the state governments the FairTax on all their purchases and services. "The power to tax is the power to destroy," Chief Justice John Marshall declared in 1819 in the famous case of **McCullough v. Maryland**. Once the federal government has the authority to hit the states with a sales tax, expect it to be imposed and then to be raised faster than the tax on citizen purchases because it will bring revenue to the feds which the states will have to collect and for which state officials will be blamed. This is a basic cost-shifting that the feds always try to do to state and local governments via unfunded mandates, but which will be considerably easier via the FairTax.

That's the core of this objection: The federal government would gain enormous power over state governments that would fundamentally rework our long-standing, stable and deeply understood system of dual sovereignty. The FairTax folks might be good salesmen—they are great salesmen in fact—but we trust the Framers of the Constitution when it comes to the value of dual sovereignty.

We note as well that over at FairTax.org—at least as late as February 2009—the proponents of the FairTax weren't exactly candid on the issue of states and the FairTax. Here's the relevant section from the sites "FAQ" display:

How are state tax systems affected, and can states adequately collect a federal sales tax?

No state is required to repeal its income tax or piggyback its sales tax on the federal tax. All states have the opportunity to collect the FairTax; states will find it beneficial to conform their sales tax to the federal tax. Most states will probably choose to conform. It makes the administrative costs of businesses in that state much lower. The state is paid a one-quarter of one percent fee by the federal government to collect the tax. For states that already collect a sales tax, this fee proves generous. A state can choose not to collect the federal sales tax, and either outsource the collection to another state, or opt to have the federal government collect it directly. If a state chooses to conform to the federal tax base, they will raise the same amount of state sales tax with a lower tax rate— in some cases more than 50 percent lower— since the FairTax base is broader than their current tax base. States may also consider the reduction or elimination of property taxes by keeping their sales tax rate at or near where it is currently. Finally, conforming states that are part of the FairTax system will find collection of sales tax on Internet and mail-order retail sales greatly simplified.

Right. A piece of cake and an obvious choice for the states, correct?

Not at all, and not just because of the core ideological attachment to sovereignty.

All 50 states have developed unique state tax systems that reflect their long evolved cultural and political heritages, systems which reflect values and carefully constructed compromises. Each of these systems deal in one way or another with two issues near and dear to most citizens' hearts: education and public safety. The debates over how to pay for both are always intense and almost never-ending, reflecting the importance of both. The delicate compromises involved in these choices are often embedded deeply in the state revenue codes and the tax collection systems. A wrecking ball approach to the 50 systems will produce instant and deeply divisive controversy.

Finally, the FairTax folks breezily conjure up new state administrative authorities ("SSTAs") to collect the new federal and state fair taxes, the State Sales Tax Administering Authorities. States that have had trouble running DMVs and child service departments instantly have to staff up to effectively categorize all families (for Prebate purposes) and collect all sales taxes—and enforce the laws—without an IRS to lean on. No cost estimates are advanced. No estimate of size and organization are proposed. No rule books exist.

This wild conjuring of whole new agencies operating more efficiently than any ever has is just another example of the FairTax's reliance on the instant invention of systems whenever it needs them. But anyone who watches state governments closely knows how difficult they are to manage or change, even under the best of circumstances.

The states aren't going to buy the new system. There are enormous built-in obstacles to change, and the states aren't going to rush to greet their new federal masters at the door. In fact, the moment that the FairTax became more than a pipe dream, the state legislatures and governors would begin to bring their considerable political muscle to bear to shut it down. That they haven't already is simply proof that no one charged with the serious business of running governments takes the FairTax seriously. Indeed, Democrats and proponents of big government generally have to be secretly applauding the work of FairTax enthusiasts as it drains real reform of energy and resources.

Chapter 22

Will the States Choose To Become a State Sales Tax Administrating Authority ?

———— ∞∞∞ ————

The FairTax folk are hoping and expecting that all or most all of the states agree to become part of the replacement system for the disappeared IRS by agreeing to set up "State Sales Tax Administrating Authorities" ("STAA") which will be compensated by a very small portion of the federal receipts collected.

If a state declines to establish a STAA, the federal Department of the Treasury would assume the tasks that would go along with collecting taxes from such a massive new tax program. Meet the new IRS, though it will be called something different. It would certainly remain housed under the Treasury, the current home of the Internal Revenue Service.

As noted before, a STAA would have to (1) annually register every legal resident of its state, (2) create software to maintain the registration of every legal resident of its state, and (3) collect federal sales taxes from virtually every business in its state. And there would be fifty of these plus an agency somewhere to address territories of Puerto Rico, Guam, etc.

Or a state could elect to let the feds administer their own taxes.

We think most analysts will urge governors and legislators to steer far from the STAAs. There are many downsides and absolutely no serious upside to a decision to establish a STAA. The keys: There is no significant profit to be made by a state and there is both the possibility of a significant financial and political losses as the result of the initial and annual registration of lawful residents as well as the demands of ongoing collections. There is also the possibility of failure to accomplish a confidential and fraud-free registration and the accompanying political and legal fallout. Elected officials aren't in the habit of taking on very big risks for very little return. Because it is impossible under our Constitution to compel the states to take on these burdens, expect the Treasury to end up holding most or all of the bags across the 50 states.

The FairTax proponents know that they cannot force the states to take up the many challenges of FairTax administration, so they offer a tiny fee: One quarter of one percent of all federal sales tax revenues collected will remain with the state. This is the same amount offered to companies to prepare monthly FairTax forms under the FairTax. The companies need only collect the tax and send a check with a form to get their pay-off, but, the states have massive additional responsibilities. The possibility of a state or many states losing zillions of dollars performing this role looms very, very large. Compare whatever the potential proceeds at ¼ of one percent to the cost of the actual responsibilities:

- Initial registration of every legal resident including determination of legal status
- Continuing registration of every legal resident including births, deaths, address changes and family unit changes
- Collection of the FairTax and remittance to the feds
- Auditing of residents and businesses for compliance with the FairTax

To accomplish these tasks, employees and software would need to be developed to administer the FairTax. The software would have to be sufficiently robust to accomplish all of the tasks required and to maintain the privacy of families . ("Sufficiently robust" may not do justice to a system which in California alone, would have to track about 30+ million legal residents and exclude millions of illegal residents.) Bureaucracies would need to be created and expanded to accomplish these tasks. These tasks would require the state to manage perhaps thousands and thousands of full and part time employees.

Because registration as a legal recipient brings a Prebate check, we also note that states will have very little incentive to distinguish between legal and illegal residents, and quite an incentive to lean towards declaring a resident legal as the state and local community will benefit from the flow of Prebates , but will be pressed by the presence of illegal aliens facing massive price hikes but not receiving any Prebate.

There's also the inherent conflict-of-interest in making states the overseers of a tax system that will tax state purchases.

We expect that the states will first oppose the passage of the FairTax and the repeal of the 16th Amendment, and if overpowered by the (as yet nonexistent) surge of support for the FairTax, will sit out the implementation phase, choosing instead to maintain and perfect its in-place approach to taxation, including the variety of income/property/corporate and sales taxes presently used across the country.

Elected officials like low risk approaches to their political futures. Signing on to the runaway train that is the FairTax is a huge gamble with a low payout, which is why so few governors and presidential candidates have signed on. Congressmen don't mind a cost-free "me too" since it generates so little blowback at this point, but high profile electeds know that opposition researchers among Democrats are just waiting for the big, fat target on the back of anyone saying "yes" to the FairTax outside a Republican primary. That's just the political reality, and FairTax arguments that count on the states eagerly rushing in to pick up the role of the IRS are undermined by the great, collective common sense about re-election that unites most politicians across the ideological spectrum.

"What's in it for me?" each and every governor and state legislator will ask. The famous WIIFM proposition! And the answer will be a great many negatives and very little—if any—positives.

Chapter 23

Does a State Want to Give Up Its State Income Tax System?

―⊸∞⊷―

If a state wants to preserve its state income tax system, the best possibility of doing so would be to stop the FairTax. As discussed earlier, every state that has an income tax puts such high reliance on the Internal Revenue Service for statutory language, regulations and enforcement, that the preservation of a state income tax system without the Internal Revenue Service would be extremely expensive. The underlying structure of the administrative system would have to be built to a strength similar to the Internal Revenue Service to maintain an income tax system. As noted earlier, the cost of this to each state would be monumental. Teams would need to be hired and taught to do effective auditing at much higher levels than states commonly participate today.

What are the consequences of either abandoning the state income tax or changing the state sales tax, or both? We have to make assumptions here to illustrate the difficulties ahead, but they are fair ones. Let's assume that at least one state does adopt the FairTax, abandons its income tax and adopts the FairTax sales tax methodology and taxes all products for final consumption. Let's assume the new sales tax rate for this state is 7 percent. (Note, in Los Angeles, the current sales tax, with exemptions, is virtually at 10 percent.)

Does a state want to have a single taxing methodology and one that is so clearly regressive? Does a state want to have some of its richest residents not paying significant income taxes to their state? Does a state want to be in a position where when it needs to raise more revenues, the only source of such revenues is an increase to the state sales tax which will impact rich and poor alike? We think most elected officials across the ideological spectrum will say no.

The authors note here that there is an existing study entitled *Fiscal Federalism: The National FairTax and the States* from Beacon Hill Institute at Suffolk University which reaches a conclusion that most states could adopt the FairTax methodology of sales taxation and lower their sales tax rates. To accomplish the magic of lowering the sales tax rate and raising additional revenue, the study assumes that each state will adopt the much wider sales tax methodology of the FairTax extending the sales tax to such goods as food and such services as urgent medical care. (This study also appears to assume that government employees will not have their salaries increased by the amount of federal and state taxes previously withheld. Anyone who has ever sat down in a municipal union negotiation would find the concept of all private sector employees receiving their federal and state withholding as increased salary while the state employees would not receive this benefit to be the basic material for stand-up comedy.)

But neither this study nor any other study of the FairTax even attempts to predict the post-FairTax behavioral changes and revenue impacts on state treasuries with anything approaching sophisticated planning. The budgets of most of the states surpass the budgets of most countries of the world, and the services funded by those budgets are among the most necessary to civil society—police and fire, of course, but also education and transportation The proponents of the FairTax are urging Congress to simply "roll the dice" and see what comes of it.

If the FairTax proposal ever becomes more than a debating club and a profit center, the states and their many constituencies will rightly ridicule the movement and its backers as the fiscal equivalent of medical quackery.

Chapter 24

There Is No Free Lunch Or Free Tax: The Costs of The FairTax

———⊗⊗⊗———

The FairTax folk have a study—they have lots of studies—that asserts that Americans would save $346 billion dollars from the switch to the FairTax. This study includes the value of time spent preparing tax returns, a hypothetical "saving" subject to extraordinary manipulation via the assumptions invented to support it.

This study is also silent on transition and maintenance costs of the new systems required to establish and operate the FairTax. Actually, there appears to be no studies which attempt to determine the costs of creating and maintaining a State Sales Tax Administrating Authority.

The transition activities and costs associated with a switch to a FairTax would include the following:

- Continued operation of the current federal income tax system for several years following FairTax implementation, at a reduced but significant cost. Taxes owed under the old system will still be owed and audits/collection activities will have to be maintained or the approach of the FairTax will unleash the greatest era of tax noncompliance in history.
- Creation of:
  a. Up to 50 separate State Sales Tax Administrating Authority software programs to register and track a total of more than 300,000,000 legal residents, while continuously

adding newborns, subtracting deaths, tracking moves and other family unit changes. (Each program must be able to interface with the new systems being created by the Social Security Administration.)

b. Up to 50 separate State Sales Tax Administrating Authority software programs to receive, review and audit monthly sales tax collections and reports.

c. A Social Security software program and support employees with the ability to interact with each of the 50 different state Sales Tax Administrating Authorities and distribute approximately 114,000,000 Prebate checks or direct deposits a month

d. A Social Security software system and support employees to collect, monitor, review and audit self employment forms from the tens of millions of independent businesses in the United States.

The State Sales Tax Administrating Authorities and the Social Security Administration are looking at massive gear-up programs and massive permanent operations. These state authorities would need to initially hire sufficient employees and lease a sufficient number of locations to annually register every legal resident in each state. The employment plan would need to provide for well supervised part time workers to initially register and subsequently annually register all of these legal residents. (The FairTax calls for a single annual registration date and, therefore, a significant part of the work force would need to be seasonal.) The full time staff would need to perform auditing of the information submitted to document both legal status and family allowance. Part of this process would include a system for verifying every social security number with the Social Security Administration.

The state authorities would also be required to register virtually every business in each state, and collect monthly and annual forms and checks from each of these entities. Forms mean auditors. Lots and lots of auditors.

The Social Security Administration would need to expand its capabilities to cover the issuance of an additional 114 million checks per month. This is more than twice the number of current checks being issued every month, and of course the current workload isn't going anywhere either.

The Social Security Administration would also have to create an employment base to receive and audit millions of annual self-employment filings from self-employed individuals. Under the FairTax these small businesses would be filing what would be the equivalent of an income tax return annually for purposes of indicating the amount of Social Security credits earned by their employees. The Social Security Administration would need new teams of auditors to cover these millions of businesses, and a new system of auditing. Keep fixed firmly in your mind that the more lifetime income you report to the Social Security Administration, the more retirement benefits you receive. The Social Security system currently benefits from the taxpayer reporting every possible deduction in his or her tax return in an effort to reduce income taxes. This keeps down artificial and fraudulent claims to have made income, even though that claim would increase retirement benefits years down the road. This barrier to fraud is eliminated with a FairTax as the self employed would have higher Social Security income and therefore higher Social Security benefits by reporting higher income and no offsetting income taxes. Where self-employed people have an incentive to declare all income and no tax is leveled on net income but retirement benefits flow from it, a new era of fraud opens.

The FairTax folk provide no estimates with respect to the cost of the software systems and personnel additions discussed above, even though they are quick to proclaim the $346 billion in savings from implementation of the FairTax. We aren't even convinced of even the possibility of successfully building and effectively administering a system mailing 114,000,000 Prebates to a highly mobile population, but if such a possibility exists, it will come with a very high price tag.

Finally, we note that the FairTax proposes to fire or retire hundreds of thousands of federal and state workers from the existing systems, while hiring and training hundreds of thousands of new workers for the new systems.

We note the unhappy history of massive hiring programs for new government agencies. Look at the history of the Transportation Security Administration ("TSA"), formed in the aftermath of the attacks of 9/11 even given the urgent mission of protecting American travelers.

The TSA employs 43,000. In the first six years of its history, it is estimated that more than 67,000 people came and left the agency as it struggled to find its workforce. The training costs for the 43,000 have been staggering, and costs sunk into the 67,000 who left.

We respect the work of the TSA, and note the difficulty of maintaining vigilance and professionalism in the face of the surging crowds of American and foreign travelers streaming through the nation's transportation nodes. It is a hard thing to staff up and maintain professionalism.

But it will be harder still by a matter of many degrees to find the skill sets necessary to manage this vast new FairTax apparatus given the level of analytical and software skills required. The TSA has been searching for people to run the machines and systems associated with checkpoints and homeland security. Where travelers are obliged to come to the inspection point and submit to the methods and inspectors. The state authorities and expanded Social Security Administration will need to find people who can handle the math and the fraud flowing in from 300 million Americans plus all the legal residents. And there will be little in the way of quietly moving lives and docile customers.

Implementing and administrating a FairTax would be, if it even possible, an incredibly difficult and expensive task.

Chapter 25

Years 2 Through 200

———— ✺ ————

So some agency or agencies are going to register 300,000,000 Americans, create highly efficient tracking and verification systems using software not yet developed, protect everyone's privacy, audit all businesses collecting the new sales taxes and get the tax money to the right people. They also have to get the Prebates calculated and out the door.

Can they do it again the next year? And the next year? And the next year?

There's much more than a touch of unreality to the enthusiasms of the FairTax folk for how all this is going to proceed. Not many of them, we think, have been around government much, or ever overseen the establishment and start up of a complex organization.

Did we mention most of the state and federal employees in the country are union members, and that their hiring and firing is a complicated business? (Long ago and far away, Hugh was the General Counsel and then Deputy Director of the U.S. Office of Personnel Management, the successor agency to the Civil Service Commission. He is always amused by grandiose restructuring plans because during his time at the agency, a senior official there couldn't fire a secretary after over two years of trying.)

We ignore the optimistic scenarios put forward concerning implementation by the FairTax folk. But we do note that they admit even the beginning of implementation is years and years off because the starting gun doesn't sound until the 16th Amendment is repealed. From the FAQ section of FairTax.org:

> *Could we end up with both the FairTax and an income tax?*
>
> *No current supporter of the FairTax would support the FairTax unless the entire income tax is repealed. Moreover, concurrent with the repeal of the income tax, a constitutional amendment repealing the 16th Amendment and prohibiting an income tax will be pushed through Congress for ratification by the states (filed as HJR 16 in the 110th Congress).*

So we are a decade off at least given the history of most other constitutional amendments.

We assume technology will continue to advance and so some aspects of the FairTax set-up will become easier, but so will concerns over privacy continue to increase. It will be easier to collect data and track people, but more and more people aren't going to want all that data in one place, and they certainly aren't going to be in a hurry to turn all the data on themselves over to the states to keep in one easy-to-access-registry.

Assume somehow the 16th Amendment gets repealed, the FairTax gets authorized, it survives numerous legal challenges, and it is time to build the system. We remind you of what's involved:

1. Every legal resident must
    a. have or obtain a Social Security Number;
    b. Register with respect to residence and Prebate with either the Social Security Administration or the State Sales Tax Administrating Authority for the state in which they live;
    c. File the appropriate forms with respect to any moves, deaths etc. with respect to receiving the Prebate.

2. Every state must:
    a. determine whether it is going to maintain its current system of taxation or change their taxation system to either comport with or be an appendage to the FairTax

b. determine if it will establish a "STAA", and no matter whether it says yes or no—we predict in Chapter 22, most or all say no—each of the 45 states with its own sales tax will have to determine how to adjust, administer, and collect taxes on a parallel system.

c. if it becomes a STAA, negotiate a contract with the federal government to become a STAA and create a bureaucracy to both register every lawful resident of their state and obtain a specific list of initial information about each lawful resident.

d. if it becomes a STAA, expand or create a division of their STAA to register every seller of goods and services for consumption in their respective state.

e. if it becomes a STAA, build a technical infrastructure, including software which can communicate with the Social Security Administration and maintain privacy to administer the initial and continuing locations of all legal residents. The technical infrastructure must include a tax collection process which is secure and efficient and which can interface with all registered sellers.

f. if it becomes a STAA, build or expand an audit capability to enforce all of the rules and regulations of the FairTax including the legitimacy of all legal residents, the rules regarding residency, and the collection of the FairTax.

3. The Social Security Administration of the federal government must:
    a. expand its organization to be able to timely issue Social Security numbers for all legal residents
    b. develop technology and create a bureaucracy to interface with up to fifty state software systems to verify every social security number provided for purposes of the Prebate
    c. develop technology and create a bureaucracy to deliver over 114 million prebate checks per month to the correct addresses or bank accounts. Both the bureaucracy and the technology will need to be able to accommodate and

      manage ***millions*** of monthly changes of residence and situation with respect to the Prebate family rules

   d. develop technology and create a bureaucracy to manage the filing of Social Security information which will now come directly from both the self employed and corporations.

   e. develop technology and create a bureaucracy to effectively audit social security filings for employees and the self employed to insure that individuals are not being added to the company rolls and that all deductions are being claimed with respect to calculating self employment income.

     There are lots of other functions that will need to expand dramatically, such as the border/customs enforcement operations, both inbound and outbound, because of the FairTax's enormous impact on exports and imports.

     Here's another practical problem: No state will be willing to invest in the planning, software, and reorganization to implement necessary to implement the FairTax until repeal of the 16th Amendment—on which it all hangs—and passage of implementing legislation through Congress was achieved. Repeal is highly unlikely, but even if it advanced rapidly towards passage still few if any states would expend crucial resources on start-up planning as amending the Constitution is an "all or nothing" proposition, and failure by even one state means starting all over again. The prospect of getting the necessary amendment(s) to the states is remote, but even then passage by 38 of the states would be a longer shot still. No start-up dollars would be expended on this far-fetched fantasy until it actually came to pass, and then the prospect of chaos would itself slow down the ratification process.

     The chaos that follows implementation would be real.

     Focus, for example, on California.

     California has more than 36 million residents in more than 13 million housing units. Implementation would require that every family member be registered and that registration indicate the family unit to receive the Prebate. The enormity of this undertaking is beyond the capacity of most of us to understand, and the complexity of determining "family unit" almost unbelievably difficult to organize rules around. Ozzie and Harriet are easy enough—until Ricky turns 18, but decides to stay at home, until he moves out, only to move back in with his girlfriend.

Get it?

Divide the registration process into two separate events. First, is the initial registration. Second is the on-going registration.

The staffing for the original registration of all lawful residents would have to include significant numbers of one-time and seasonal employees. It would also need to include management personnel capable of managing a new, untrained and short term work force. That work force would need to deal in literally dozens of languages and master the underlying rules of the FairTax with respect to common residence, definition of family members and excluded individuals.

How many Californians would be required and how long would it take to correctly register 36 million people in 13 million separate residences?

Each individual contacted will need a social security number and will have to prove legal residency. The fraud at sign-up will be huge, and almost certainly a significant percentage of initial registrations should occur in face-to-face meetings. Start doing the math on the minutes necessary to run the start-up. Since the bigger the family the larger the Prebate, the government is going to have to count heads, or birth certificates very, very carefully. And every birth and death and move changes the Prebate process.

Now, imagine an agency at least the size of DMV handling far more transactions every day than DMV does in a month as the system goes from start-up to ongoing operations.

The IRS currently runs a far less extensive, far less intrusive process, one that can rely on the threat of audit for compliance and which generally only has to send out refund checks based upon affirmative demands for them, accompanied by persuasive paperwork. Even then, lots of fraud occurs, and lots of mistakes. One of the reasons the IRS is so unpopular is because it is asked to do so much with relatively minimal resources. Mistakes happen.

The FairTax proposal calls for the Internal Revenue Service to complete their cycle of audits underway at the time of adoption and then to go out of business. They are put on a relatively short going-out-of-business schedule, one that strikes practitioners such as Hank as wildly unrealistic, and former federal employees like Hugh as wildly amusing. The IRS, like all federal agencies, lumbers forward. It has an enormous number of things to get done and even though it is generally staffed by competent, well-meaning professionals, like every other governmental agency in the world, it isn't built for speed.

It is hard to turn such an organization from its long established culture and practices, but , harder still to replace it with magic and even the best of intentions. Its employees are professionals and many are union members with rights about relocation and bumping into other jobs. Most are dedicated and hard working professionals who deserve the rights they have accrued under contacts fairly bargained for. And they will get them.

The idea of a quick transition is just more laughable rhetoric from FairTax proponents who count on observers never taking the details seriously enough to raise fundamental questions about logistics.

Of course, any tax-and-collection scheme isn't going to run without massive numbers of trained personnel. FairTax proponents obscure this reality by asserting unbelievable time frames for doing impossible things. Just part of the same fast-talking scam, which is never more obvious than when we contemplate the actual sign-up and Prebate send-out envisioned after that darned 16th Amendment goes away.

Chapter 26

Killing Social Security Via The FairTax

―∞∞―

The FairTax proposal presents three serious threats to the Social Security system as it exists today.

Under the current Social Security regimen, employees' social security taxes are withheld from their payroll checks. While some think of the Social Security as a savings plan, today, we rightly refer to the collection of social security as a payroll tax. We often need to recall that Social Security is essentially designed to be a "safety net" pension program for all Americans. To receive Social Security payments in retirement, an employee must pay into the Social Security system throughout his or her working life. Employers must also make matching contributions equal to the amounts of Social Security taxes paid by the employee.

Self employed individuals pay their personal Social Security taxes through their federal income tax returns. The calculation of their Social Security payment requirement is based upon the taxable income from their business. Self employed individuals pay both the employer and employee share of the self employment taxes.

The current system creates a direct relationship between payments to the federal government of Social Security taxes and qualification for Social Security benefits. This in turn creates a situation where there is no incentive to add individuals to employment roles for the sole purpose of qualifying for Social Security. It is simply too expensive a decision to add a brother to the payroll as it requires the payment of salary, payroll taxes and federal and state income tax withholding.

Under the FairTax, the payment of Social Security taxes by employee, employer and self-employed disappears. At the moment employment is decoupled from the taxes necessary to pay the benefits, an incentive is created to add a fraudulent employee (Brother Bob) to the payroll sheets as this does not cost a nickel but qualifies Brother Bob for a benefit down the road. Brother Bob will now get Social Security credit toward future benefits and it will not cost his employer (brother) a penny. He just adds Bob to the employee list and writes down a big salary. While the Social Security Administration could be charged with auditing to find this fraud, finding this needle in the hay stack would be extremely difficult.

For the self employed, currently Social Security taxes are calculated based upon taxable income from the enterprise. Because the self employed individual pays income taxes on the earnings from his business, his incentive is to minimize expenses and maximize earnings. Under current law, virtually no one overstates his self employment earnings in order to increase benefits in the retirement years—it is too expensive a proposition as the overstatement of earnings drives a higher income tax.

Under the FairTax, the goal of the self employed would be to maximize the income reported from self employment in order to maximize Social Security benefits in the out years. As there would be no income tax post adoption of the FairTax, there would be no reason to claim all of the expenses of the enterprise, as claiming expenses would reduce Social Security payments to the self employed individual. Without doubt, this "subtlety" would increase the costs of Social Security payments by the federal government dramatically.

Self employed individuals currently receive social security benefits based upon their self employment income. Self employment income for social security purposes is currently calculated in a manner identical to the calculation of taxable income for federal income tax purposes. The FairTax replaces this system with a definition of self employment income as gross payments for taxable property or services less the sum of gross payments for taxable property or services and wages.

This appears to be a mistake of significant proportion.

Under the definition, any business selling products for re-sale would have no gross payments received for taxable property and therefore no self employment income, regardless of the business's actual income. This would exclude many self-employed individuals of the opportunity to collect Social Security benefits. However, it would not prevent these individuals from paying the FairTax to fund other people's Social Security.

Who would these self employed individuals be who would be excluded from receiving benefits under Social Security. They would be the owners of the companies that made the parts for trucks, raised the corn for corn flakes and or caught the fish for the local restaurant. This is a significant segment of our society. In an instant giant holes are torn in the Social Security blanket.

Beyond the enormously problematic incentives instituted by operation of the FairTax, there are also enormous burdens imposed on the agency within the Department of the Treasury that is already charged with making sure senior citizens get their benefits and the disabled their due: The Social Security Administration, or "SSA."

The SSA is not remotely prepared to perform the roles assigned it via the FairTax. An already burdened agency faces a massive "scale-up" in employees, costs, complexity and execution tasks. We doubt very much that this can be done without injury to its core mission, which is a hugely important one since it is a "safety net" function. One of the great political miscalculations of the FairTax proposal is the repeated reliance on an SSA on steroids. Older Americans have time and again punished any politician who wants to mess with SSA. All of the FairTax folks' protests that no harm will come to SSA will fall on deaf ears as AARP organizes to defeat the FairTax. Any politicians standing around the FairTax when America's senior citizens get moving are in for big political trouble.

And AARP won't be making it up. The FairTax really does threaten the smooth operation of SSA by loading it with new and difficult tasks.

The FairTax requires that the Social Security Administration to perform four separate and difficult roles to implement the FairTax.

The first role is to provide new Social Security cards to millions of Americans (most under the age of five) so that these legal residents can receive the Prebate. The opportunity for fraud in the receipt of a Social Security card in this initial rush of registration is high. From the applicant's viewpoint, a Social Security card means a significant monthly check. The SSA has to expect it will become a fraud magnet overnight far beyond what any other government agency has ever been in terms of size and temptation level.

Next, the SSA will have to develop some extraordinarily complex systems in a very short period of time. The system requirements of the FairTax call for the Social Security Administration to verify the Social Security number of every legal resident before the first dollar of Prebates can be paid. This will require integrating the Social Security information systems with the separate sales tax administrating authorities that are established. Each state would need a system that was integrated with the SSA and the SSA would need to be able to move payments from state to state as citizens moved from state to state. The dollars involved in the verification process with respect to duplicate Social Security numbers, name changes (think marriage), errors and fraud would take a new army of trained Social Security administrators.

The third aspect of the Social Security Administration would be the actual payment of the monthly Prebate. Today, the Social Security system sends just over 55 million checks every month. To do this, it employs 80,000 people, has over 1300 offices, receives over 42 million office visits and logs over 65 million annual 800 number telephone calls.

The United States has about 114 million households. The FairTax would require the Social Security Administration to create an entirely new data base for all 114 million households. This data base would be completely separate from the data base currently used for Social Security retirement and disability payments. This new system would have to be updated daily for all of the issues that the current Social Security base is updated and a few more such as a child leaving the family residence to move into a new apartment. The Prebate bureaucracy and operation requirement for the Prebate would cost at least as much as the current social security system to operate and as the number of checks per month is a bit more than two times the current monthly number, perhaps a great deal more. The number of office visits from the general population could be significantly greater than the current number of office visits. The picture is of a vast new bureaucracy built on the already enormous foundations of the SSA. What was the purpose of getting rid of the IRS anyway?

Neal Boortz downplays these obvious problems of scale, writing in one of his books that "We submit to you that any government that is already issuing 48 million checks covering Social Security recipients alone won't have a big problem issuing FairTax rebates to every head of household in the country."

We submit to you that Neal has never run anything but a studio. The idea of a tripling of functions being no big deal ought to cause every dispassionate observer to pause and ask themselves what can they trust in this big pitch?

Finally, the SSA would have to massively expand its audit capacity because under the FairTax, self-employed Social Security filings would be made directly to the SSA. An annual filing would have to be made by each self employed taxpayer reporting income for the purpose of calculating future Social Security benefits. An annual filing would also have to be made reporting the Social Security earnings of each employee by every business in the United States. The Social Security Administration currently relies on the requirement of payroll taxes to insure that extra individuals are not added to payrolls for the purpose of collecting social security benefits. Without the Internal Revenue Service and without payroll withholding, the dynamic of ensuring a fraud free social security system would be lost. An entire system of auditing and enforcement would therefore need to be developed and implemented by the SSA because the desire for social security benefits isn't going to diminish among all the recently retired Boomers. They are going to want their checks, and future retirees will want theirs as well, which means auditing the self-employed for accuracy in their annual filings with the SSA. Meet the new IRS.

The SSA on steroids is one of the most obvious weakness of the FairTax fantasy. When the FairTax folk find three or four retired Social Security Administrators to endorse this wild scheme, then it should be taken seriously.

Chapter 28

Remember 1896

⣷⣊⣶

William Jennings Bryan was three times the nominee of the Democratic Party, and on the occasion of his first nomination, he gave a fiery speech demanding the end of the Gold Standard and the implementation of what was known as "bimetallism," which meant in practice that the money supply would expand through the widespread use of silver. Bryan concluded his acceptance speech at the Democratic Convention that year with one of the most famous phrases in the history of American politics:

> *Having behind us the producing masses of this nation and the world, supported by the commercial interests, the laboring interests and the toilers everywhere, we will answer their demand for a gold standard by saying to them: You shall not press down upon the brow of labor this crown of thorns, you shall not crucify mankind upon a **cross of gold.***

A wonderful phrase, that—"a cross of gold." The "Silverites," as proponents of bimetallism were known, were thrilled and their cause, they thought, assured of victory.

Bryan lost, of course, and lost again in 1900 and 1908. The crusade for silver never captured the enthusiasm of the country in the way it captured the enthusiasm of its devotees. Indeed, that enthusiasm may have blinded Bryan and his followers to the precarious nature of their

137

appeal: It just didn't motivate majorities and it seemed very, very risky to non-enthusiasts.

The FairTax enthusiasts of the early 21st century are a lot like the Silverites of the late 19th century. They are smart, organized, and passionate. They are, in a word, **_certain_** of the rightness of their cause and of the inevitability of their victory. They may even have their Bryan in the person of former Arkansas Governor Mike Huckabee, who is a passionate defender of the FairTax, and who found himself rewarded in the 2008 Iowa caucuses because the caucuses amplified the enthusiasm of the FairTax folk. (Governor Huckabee also benefited from the support of other groups such as evangelicals and especially the home-schooling community, but no one denies the FairTax movement's role in his come-from-nowhere win in the caucuses.)

But Governor Huckabee's appeal quickly wore out—he was never a serious candidate in New Hampshire, Michigan or any major primary outside of the south. His campaign was one that rested primarily on the votes of evangelical Christians, and mostly southern Evangelical Christians. There aren't enough supporters of the FairTax to make a difference outside of a small state using a highly unusual election methodology like Iowa's very distinctive caucus approach. Out on the open field of a big state, the FairTax voters matter, but not much. There just aren't that many of them.

Nor will there ever be. Before other GOP pied pipers arrive to urge the party to follow the FairTax music, we hope center-right Republicans and conservatives generally will do a little electoral math.

In 2006, the Joint Economic Committee of the United States issued the following schedule:

Progression in Federal Income Tax Payments

Size of AGI	Number of Returns	Refundable Portion of EITC & CTC US$000	Total Income Tax Amount Including Refundable Credits US$000	Average Income Tax Including Refundable Credits
All returns	130,423,626	($43,125,048)	$704,892,440	$5,405
No AGI	1,813,840	($362,509)	($283,931)	($157)
$1 under $5,000	11,697,628	($1,723,064)	($1,650,106)	($141)
$5,000 under $10,000	12,503,409	($6,781,432)	($6,000,982)	($480)
$10,000 under $15,000	12,002,004	($10,950,887)	($8,200,228)	($683)
$15,000 under $20,000	11,293,967	($10,104,164)	($4,699,431)	($416)
$20,000 under $25,000	9,831,150	($6,690,557)	$1,583,529	$161
$25,000 under $30,000	8,541,753	($3,526,262)	$7,509,778	$879
$30,000 under $40,000	13,957,257	($2,035,283)	$27,702,535	$1,985
$40,000 under $50,000	10,452,444	($610,965)	$34,024,248	$3,255
$50,000 under $75,000	17,372,492	($275,318)	$93,980,875	$5,410
$75,000 under $100,000	9,542,599	($56,318)	$84,196,798	$8,823
$100,000 under $200,000	8,878,643	($8,289)	$163,334,118	$18,396
$200,000 under $500,000	1,999,016	$0	$120,711,552	$60,385
$500,000 under $1,000,000	356,140	$0	$60,180,642	$168,980
$1,000,000 or more	181,283	$0	$132,503,043	$730,918

Source: JEC Calculations based on SOI Data for TY2003 - SOI Bulletin Fall 2005.
Notes: (1) Detail may not add due to rounding; (2) Figures in parenthesis are negative amounts.

Several facts included in this schedule should be lost on no one:

- 40 percent of federal income tax filers pay no federal income taxes
- 84 percent of federal income tax filers pay $5410 or less in federal income taxes
- A single taxpayer earning less than $8950 need not file a federal income tax return and is not included in this schedule.
- Millions of voters pay only Social Security taxes.

While the FairTax issue may resonate deeply within a relatively small percentage of the Republican Party, taxpayers who do not pay any federal income taxes or who pay very, very little in federal income taxes are not going to be persuaded that the FairTax is important to them, and many will likely assume that either (1) this is simply a new way for them to be taxed, or (2) this is a scheme for the wealthy to avoid paying taxes. Most likely both. They will hear the part about a 30 percent sales tax on everything, and they will see the very wealthy dancing at the FairTax rallies. A GOP already dangerously close to losing touch with the lower middle class will be at risk of writing off the entire middle class in a stroke.

There's a reason why only Governor Huckabee embraced the FairTax in 2008. He was way behind Senator McCain, Governor Romney, and Mayor Giuliani and needed the support of anyone he could get. When he signed on to the FairTax he enlisted a small army of volunteers on his side in Iowa, and they came through for him. FairTax rhetoric also protected the governor against attacks from the Club for Growth and others who accused him of having been a tax-and-spend governor during his decade in the Arkansas state house.

No other major GOP candidate came close to embracing the FairTax though all of them—Giuliani, McCain, Romney and Thompson— spoke favorably of tax reform. What they and their staffs know—what every political reporter in the country knows—is that the FairTax is a poison pill that will kill any candidate who swallows it when general election times comes around.

It is that simple. The FairTax is political suicide for the GOP.

Chapter 29

The Debate Ahead

Yes, we know it is coming. At least we hope it is.

Many of the issues addressed in this book are not addressed by the proponents of the FairTax. *The FairTax Book* devotes a lot of time to straw men arguments, but none at all to many of the most obvious objections to the scheme. *Fair Tax: The Truth* is more of the same. Serious proposals should answer the most serious charges against them.

And not with hyperbole or misdirection.

Neal Boortz conducts a lot of the FairTax band, and does so with the skill of a long time talk show host using many of the tricks of the trade. Our favorite example of Neal's skill in setting the debate in terms he prefers comes from his discussion of the 23/30 divide. We return to it now in anticipation of the debates ahead, though we genuinely wonder whether the FairTax folk are going to want to engage in any serious debates.

This is from Boortz's second book:

"Our opponents have argued that we are misleading America on the Fair Tax rate. If you should ever hear or read that the Fair Tax proponents are lying, that we're trying to put one over on you, you can bet the next sentence will go something like this: Those Fair Tax frauds say the sales tax will be 23 percent when it's obviously 30 percent

*No doubt most of these critics fully understand the game they
are playing. They know that if they can convince the American
people that we're not telling them the whole truth, they can effectively cripple the FairTax effort - thus preserving the status quo and
in many cases their power and even their jobs."*

A bit later Neal adds::

*"So how do these opponents and skeptics come up with the 30
percent figure? By playing on the confusion that exists between an
inclusive and exclusive sales tax, that's how. This confusion is exac-
erbated by the fact that virtually every one of the forty-five states
that collect a sales tax computes that sales tax on a tax-exclusive
basis. That's the difference: the FairTax is computed on an inclusive
basis."*

There, in a nutshell, is a fine example of polemic: Attack your
opponents' motives, and assert that no one can oppose the FairTax
except on malicious or self-serving grounds, and then demand that
the language of the debate ignore the common experience of the audience—45 states describe sales taxes using "tax exclusive" language.

We think the peculiar attachment to the decidedly unusual methodology of "tax-inclusive" language is a giveaway, a sort of "poker tell"
that telegraphs the FairTax folk style of argument, which is to avoid
the biggest issues via misdirection. Arguing about the 23/30 divide
eats up a lot of time that should instead be devoted to, say, whether or
not the 16th Amendment must be repealed prior to adoption of the
FairTax, the constitutionality of the FairTax applied to state purchases,
the impact of not levying the FairTax on exports etc.

Too often we see FairTax folk refusing to answer simple questions with simple answers. Too often we hear rhetoric deployed where
uncomplicated answers ought easily to be available. And too often we
hear filibusters where concise, specific replies are necessary.

As an example of what passes for a FairTax "debate," here is the
conversation between Hugh and Governor Mike Huckabee from
February 9, 2009 when the governor appeared on Hugh's radio show.

Read through it and decide if the FairTax's most visible proponent is using the opportunity to answer questions about the FairTax:

HH: I've been reading a lot about the fair tax, because whenever I bring it up, the FairTax people just bang me because I'm not sold on it, yet. Is it your understanding, is your advocacy of the FairTax premised on the repeal of the 16th Amendment?

MH: Well, I think that would seal the deal for a lot of people. I'd like to say Congress wouldn't be so stupid as to try to impose both an income tax and a consumption tax. But watching what they're doing now, they might be that stupid. So certainly it would make sense to repeal the 16th Amendment if we had the FairTax. But frankly, Hugh, if we had the FairTax, we wouldn't be needing this kind of economic stimulus where it's just a spending grab bag.

HH: But do you think it's constitutional without an amendment, both the repeal of the 16th and a new amendment, to actually have a sales tax on state purchases of goods and services as the FairTax proposes?

MH: Well, it's certainly constitutional to have a sales tax. There's no reason that we couldn't have that. But I think the most important reason for the repeal of the 16th Amendment is to just give us a double sure check that Congress wouldn't somewhere out in the future, they wouldn't obviously try it immediately, but somewhere out in the future wouldn't try to double-tax us.

HH: Well, I do understand the fair tax people as saying we need to repeal the 16th for that reason. But I also think you need authority for a federal sales tax to be applied to state purchases. I mean, if the state of Arkansas goes out and buys trailers to house people in, I don't think the federal government has the Constitutional authority to tax that right now, do you, Governor?

MH: You know, I haven't heard a constitutional lawyer say that there was an issue about the FairTax. And so I'm not a lawyer. Thank goodness I'm not, sometimes, because I think they try to take the simplest things and make them complicated. But no question about one thing - the FairTax would transform our economy primarily [because] rather than investing a bunch of borrowed taxpayer dollars, we would see U.S. capital that is currently parked off-shore, about $13 trillion of it, come back to the U.S. And that's what we ought to be seeing.

HH: Governor, some of the other things I have discovered is that exports would not have a FairTax. So a Chevy that costs $50 thousand dollars in Michigan after it's produced would cost 23 percent less in Mexico. Is that going to fly?

MH: Well, the point is it's going to cost 23 percent less in the U.S., because you don't have the embedded corporate tax. And it also means that for the first time, an American making something is going to be on a level playing field with someone in China making something as it relates to a tax burden. That's one of the reasons that American manufacturers are going out of business. It's not just cheap labor, because part of our problem is if something's made in China, let's take a chair, that chair does not get taxed when it's leaving China, nor when it's coming into the U.S. But if it's built in North Carolina in one of the furniture companies over there, because of corporate tax, payroll tax and all of the hidden taxes that aren't even transparent to the average American, that chair has built into it 22 percent embedded tax before it ever gets to the showroom floor. And that's why the FairTax creates a transparent open tax system unlike the one we have now.

HH: But we don't assess on exports, right? So whatever rolls off the line in Detroit is going to cost 23 percent, or 30 percent, however you calculate it, more in the United States than it's going to cost in Mexico, because the embedded tax is going to be gone from both vehicles.

MH: It'll be gone, sure.

HH: But...

MH: But it also means that the American goes to purchase that with his entire paycheck. He's never had his paycheck before. No American's ever, unless he's self-employed, but even then he doesn't get it because in fact, he's paying even more money because of all the full load of Social Security that he's having to pay.

HH: But it doesn't...I'm just trying to get to understand it. It doesn't apply to exports, though. So we export without the FairTax everything we make in America, will cost 30 percent less, or 23 percent less, depending on how you calculate it, south of the border or north of the border?

MH: Well, if they purchase it in the U.S., they would pay the FairTax on it.

HH: Right, but if they don't, so a Chevy and that truck in Mexico...

MH: If they purchased it from Detroit, they purchased it in the U.S.

HH: No, I think, Governor, that the FairTax people say it doesn't apply to exports. So you ship them overseas, it's not on there.

MH: Well, I'm not sure how the transaction, where it's considered taking place. I'd have to defer to one of the economists who designed it. What I do know is that the American manufacturing system would finally be able to start competing again, which we can't do now. We would have capital brought in. And I know another thing. You wouldn't have the current system where illegals, prostitutes, pimps and people in the underground don't pay tax. And they'd start paying tax like the rest of us.

HH: And the illegals don't get the Prebate, right, Governor?

MH: Of course they don't.

HH: Doesn't that...

MH: It only goes to citizens.

HH: But then don't prices go up by 23-30 percent immediately?

MH: No, they don't. They do not go up more, because you have the embedded tax taken out. What you're currently paying...

HH: Governor, hold on, we'll come right back and I'll give you a second to answer that.

MH: Okay.

HH: Governor, as I understand it, most of the studies, even by the FairTax people, say prices are going to go up between 20-30 percent after the FairTax comes in, even after you back out the embedded taxes. It's just too many things out there. It's going to go up. But the Prebate's going to cover people. But we're not going to send the Prebate to illegals, so all the 12-20 million illegal aliens in America are going to face skyrocketing prices on food and shelter. And yet they're not going to get the Prebate to help them. Do you think that's going to fly?

MH: Well, I don't know why we would ever think that a person who has crossed this border and living here illegally should get a special tax benefit that should be going to American citizens. It's not a matter of punishing people, it's a matter of saying look, if you want to come here legally, you're going to get the benefits. If you're not here legally, you don't get the benefits.

HH: What do you think happens when we've got 12-20 million illegals who are facing 20-30 percent price hikes without any help?

MH: You know, I think some of them will decide that maybe life on the other side of the border is better. And others will then accelerate their desire to become legal and get the proper documentation.

HH: Governor, you're well known as an evangelical. Do you think it's evangelically appropriate to do a 30 percent food price hike on people who are at the margin of society?

MH: Well, I totally disagree, Hugh, that it's a 30 percent food hike, because first of all, the FairTax, in order to get to the level we're at, we are now, it was at 23 percent. 22 percent is embedded. You really have somewhat of a wash. And when I hear people say that there's going to be a 30 percent hike, it goes down to talking about whether the tax is considered after or before the purchase. But the one thing that I think everybody ought to be able to agree on, the current tax system is so complicated that the guy running the IRS now doesn't even understand it. When Timothy Geithner can't use Turbo Tax and understand how to pay his taxes, I think surely we can agree that the system we have is broken.

HH: Absolutely. It's just that I don't think the fair tax works, either, Governor. I think...I'd love to have you on for an hour about this. Maybe we can come back and just talk FairTax, but we are in agreement on the stimulus at least. On that, perhaps, we can part company in agreement?

MH: Well, we certainly are in agreement that the stimulus is a stupid idea, and hopefully, one day I'll convince you that the FairTax is better than 67,000 pages of IRS tax code.

HH: Governor Mike Huckabee, always a pleasure, welcome back, Governor, I'll look forward to having you back. Now that conversation is a perfect example of why the FairTax "debate" is so frustrating to so many of us. Almost all questions and objections are met with denials of the objective reality of the plan. To place a sales tax on everything of 30 percent is going to raise prices dramatically, and many FairTax proponents understand that.

Note that as one can see from the conversation above, within the course of a ten minute conversation, the FairTax's best known proponent claims prices will not go up even with the new sales tax because embedded taxes will be removed from prices after moments before claiming that the embedded payroll and withholding taxes would be paid to the employee so he could have 100 percent of his paycheck. This scenario is impossible and the conclusions reached from an impossible scenario are bogus.

There is a studied ambiguity in the FairTax materials on the 16th Amendment, with some of them implying that the 16th Amendment must be repealed before a FairTax is passed, while others like Governor Huckabee straddle the issue perhaps because of the obvious impossibility of getting the 16th Amendment repealed in the near or even medium-term future.

Then there's the hocus-pocus on illegals choosing to leave when all the prices go up. That's not an answer to the problem of illegal immigration, and it denies the enormous hardship that the FairTax would extract on the illegal population—and the legal population dependent upon or in any way connected to them whether children, spouses, employers, employees or communities.

We didn't even get to my questions on the after effects of a hugely advantaged export market for American goods on domestic consumption and production patterns because the governor wasn't willing to follow the line of questioning.

Governor Huckabee was careful to point out that he isn't a lawyer, but he must have stayed at a Holiday Inn the night before because he was answering these questions like a lawyer playing defense would, and it is the style of Neal Boortz and others as well.

The FairTax proposes a massive sales tax hike, and provides for a hugely unwieldy Prebate to lessen the impact of the hike on the working poor, but proponents of the FairTax deny a price rise will occur!

We know that we have lots of such frustrating conversations ahead. We don't for a moment think that the FairTax folk are going to adopt the clarity of the 30 percent measure, or deal directly with the illegal alien issue, or discuss the impact on renting versus owning a home that will follow from the adoption of their scheme.

We aren't expecting candid concessions that huge new bureaucracies are required, or that thousands of auditing agents from somewhere in the government are still going to be employed, or that there's no practical way to amend constitution to protect against dual sales and income taxes except by repeal of the 16th Amendment which is decades away from happening.

In short, while we expect some in the FairTax movement will try and refute our arguments, mostly we expect more of the same: Rhetoric that promises the sun and the moon but which only conceals one of the least considered and most toxic of public policy proposals to emerge from the conservative movement in many years.

But if they want to debate it, we are game. Send the invites to either Hank or Hugh via adler@chapman.edu or hugh@hughhewitt.com.

Chapter 30

Conclusion

―❦―

We didn't plan on becoming participants in the FairTax debate. It never struck us that a national sales tax was a very serious conversation to begin with, or as a subject worthy of a great deal of time. After all, the premise of the FairTax—that it could be applied to state and local government purchases—is wildly suspect on constitutional grounds, so Hugh shrugged it off. The false promise of simplicity in a world of super-sophisticated business transactions has always amused Hank given his background with public accounting. Both of us had very solid reasons to dismiss the premise, and thus the arguments, of the FairTax folk.

But then Hank wrote a single column on the subject and the fury of the FairTax folk was very revealing. So too were the steady stream of calls that began to roll into Hugh's shows. The reaction of the FairTax enthusiasts isn't the sort that normally accompanies policy debates. Hugh's been covering religion for a long time—in print, on television and on the radio—and the outrage from the FairTax folks reminded him of the intensity that accompanies religious debates. So too did some of the debating tactics. When Hugh would raise one of his stan-dard—and quite obvious—objections such as the deeply rooted reli-ance of millions of individuals Americans on the mortgage interest deduction or the dependence of thousands of not-for-profits on chari-table contribution deduction, the FairTax folks would exclaim "HAVE YOU READ THE BOOK?" rather than provide a straightforward answer. Demands that books be read as answers to questions is another similarity of the FairTax debate to religious dispute.

We think the FairTax is a tremendously alluring mirage, and we know its power given the awful complexity of the tax system with which we live every day.

We also know—Hank better than 99 percent of Americans—the complexity of the Internal Revenue Code, the difficulty of garnering accurate answers from the IRS answer line and on occasion, (much rarer than you would imagine) the ability of the IRS to oppress and abuse.

But we also know that the perfect quickly becomes the enemy of the good, and that while the vast majority of IRS personnel are fine and often wonderful professionals who try and do their jobs, there are plenty of horror stories to motivate a tax reform movement with the abolition of the IRS at its core.

We believe in tax reform so that, as we wrote, the federal taxing system should be complex where it needs to be in order to capture the government's fair share of complex business transactions being conducted by multi-billion dollar corporations, and simple for the ordinary taxpayer who doesn't like paying taxes but realizes he or she has to, and honestly goes about it every year in March and April.

The FairTax movement hurts the tax reform movement in the way that quack medicine hurts the real thing. The FairTax is never going to be adopted for all the reasons we discussed, and it shouldn't be adopted for all the reasons we discussed. All the effort and debate (and money) that goes into promoting this ultimately fruitless effort is wasted, and worse than wasted, is damaging to the real deal—genuine tax reform and simplification.

The FairTax "movement" is also a great danger to the Republican party, which is traditionally the party of low taxes and tax reform. As FairTax enthusiasts gain in visibility and volume—though not in serious numbers—they exert a tremendous pull on understaffed and underfunded candidates who throw in with the FairTax rhetoric in order to energize faltering or broken campaigns. This is essentially what happened with Mike Huckabee's presidential campaign in 2007 and 2008. The governor was going nowhere fast until he signed on with the FairTax folk in Iowa and they powered part of his upset victory there, where a relatively small number of committed activists can transform the idiosyncratic caucuses. (To be sure, the governor also had the assistance of significant number of evangelical Christians attracted to their shared faith, and from lovers of pretty good rock-and-roll.) But the FairTax high doesn't last because it cannot persuade significant numbers of ordinary Americans that it will meaningfully benefit them. In fact, with education, most ordinary Americans will realize the enormity of the FairTax's administrative requirements and the possibility of increased taxes post FairTax. Still more voters will see that the FairTax, represents giving up, in a great sense, significant sovereignty to the federal government. The more people pay attention, the more opposition will grow.

"What if you just got behind us," the enthusiasts say. "Then we could do it, we could make a revolution in taxation!"

No set of authors or talk show hosts are powerful enough to make a lousy idea good or to change the United States Constitution, nor do we want to.

This is where we leave you. We could never support the ability of the federal government to tax the purchases and salaries of state governments. We believe that there is a huge constitutional flaw in the FairTax and we believe that if courts were to rule otherwise, then those courts would be wrongly injuring state sovereignty. When and if the federal government can tax the states, the checks and balances between the federal government and the state will be badly damaged, probably beyond repair. This is a slippery slope to a vastly more powerful central government, one which Republicans must avoid traveling.

We also believe that any number of politically powerful organizations will fight the FairTax to the death because their constituents would be seriously hurt by its adoption. We concur with many of the specific concerns of these organizations, though not with all them. We think the combined potential state, city and federal FairTax rates by its implementation will be much, much higher than 30 percent. And finally, hiring tens of thousands of individuals to register 300 million Americans for the purpose of providing fraud free delivery of 114 million monthly checks strikes us as ludicrous.

In summary, we doubt serious people will ever take the FairTax seriously for the reasons discussed in this book. The FairTax is bad policy and bad politics, which means any necessary constitutional amendment will never get out of either the House or the Senate, much less to the states.

Even if this giant, practical objection to the FairTax is ignored, Republicans should also realize that the FairTax represents a huge expansion in the power of the federal government at the expense of the states. This is a repudiation of a core principle of the party, and one that should be summarily rejected.

Life is too short, and the pressing business of America too important, to divert time, talent or money to a cause of such suspect validity and absolutely dismal prospects.

"Read the book" you say? We reply, "Read this one first."

Acknowledgements

To Marcia and Betsy, thanks for putting up with this latest frolic and detour.

Lynne Chapman, thanks for the patience of dealing with not one but two less-than-organized professors using not two but sometimes as many as four word processing programs.

And thanks to Duane and Adam and all of the interns, Asher Burke, Danielle Howe, James Skahen and Barak Wright—who have to deal with the FairTax enthusiasts who are certain they can turn us around if they can just talk to us.

Finally, to our colleagues in the Business and Law Schools at Chapman University, thanks for a work environment that encourages engagement with the issues of the day.